# MADONNARAMA
## ESSAYS ON SEX AND POPULAR CULTURE

EDITED BY **LISA FRANK** AND **PAUL SMITH**

CLEIS
PRESS

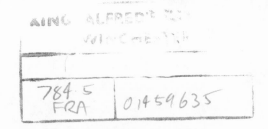
Published in the United States by Cleis Press Inc., P.O. Box 8933,
Pittsburgh, Pennsylvania 15221, and P.O. Box 14684,
San Francisco, California 94114.

Cover and interior design: Pete Ivey
Cleis logo art: Juana Alicia

Grateful acknowledgment is made to the following for permission to
reprint previously published material: "The Sound of Erotica: Pain,
Power and Pop" by Simon Frith originally appeared in *The Village
Voice*; "A Pornographic Girl" by Susie Bright originally appeared in
*San Francisco Review of Books*. Portions of this essay appeared in
Susie Bright's *Sexual Reality: A Virtual Sex World Reader* and *Susie
Sexpert's Lesbian Sex World* (Cleis Press).

Printed in the United States of America
10  9  8  7  6  5  4  3  2  1

*Library of Congress Cataloging-in-Publication Data*

Madonnarama: essays on Sex and popular culture / edited by Lisa Frank
and Paul Smith.
    p.   cm.
ISBN 0-939416-72-7 ($24.95). -- ISBN 0-939416-71-9 (pbk.) : ($9.95)
    1. Madonna, 1959–  Sex.   2. Madonna, 1959–  --Criticism and
interpretation.   3. Sexuality in popular culture.   4. Photography,
Erotic--Social aspects.   I. Frank, Lisa, 1961–  .   II. Smith, Paul, 1954–  .
HQ64.M28   1993
306.7--dc20                                        93-13296
                                                        CIP
                                                        MN

# Contents

# Introduction:
# How to Use Your
# New Madonna

## I. Ce sex event qui n'en est pas un

A huge pullout centerfold of Madonna reclining bunny-style upon the word PROVOCATIVE appeared in *Publishers Weekly* on June 15, 1992, and on the back of the picture Time-Warner Inc. announced its extensive commitment to the star's forthcoming book of erotic photos and texts, *Sex*: "Spectacular six-figure multimedia marketing campaign! Special press mailing. Tie-in with worldwide campaign for Madonna's new album. Billboard advertising in Los Angeles. Full-size stand-up Madonna easels for in-store display..." And then in the months leading up to the release of *Sex*, the public was treated to a series of stories that kept the book in the forefront of the news. In one, Madonna enlisted the help of the FBI to rescue pictures that had been pirated from the photo studio (pictures supposedly even more revealing than the ones to appear in the book); in others, the book was threatened with boycotts and censorship in the U.S. while shipments were impounded by nervous customs officers in Europe; meanwhile, Madonna herself was publicly releasing a series of leering hints about the book's contents and giving us a preview of sorts by appearing in "risqué" photospreads in both *Vanity Fair* and *Vogue*.

*Sex* was released, then, to the kind of media hoopla that publicists usually only dream of. Reviews were timed to appear with—or even days before—the book. No serial with a decent subscriber base failed to address it, and a few even gave it front cover exposure. Suddenly *Sex* was everywhere, on mainstream TV and radio, in magazines and newspapers, at academic conferences, in the gay press and the music press. There was, consequently, rampant popular curiosity: everyone wanted to see *Sex*, said they'd seen *Sex*, or refused to see *Sex*.

Measuring 10 1/4 by 13 inches and weighing in at nearly three pounds, the book is big even physically. Fabien Baron, art director at *Harper's Bazaar*, designed the book with textual assistance from ex-*Interview* editor Glenn O'Brien who helped Madonna to "clarify her feelings." Steven Meisel, doyen of fashion photography, made the photos. Each serial-numbered *Sex* is one hundred and twenty-eight cardboard pages of photographs (winnowed from over twenty thousand frames) and also features chunks of hand-written text—all of, by, and about the same subject, who is nude on almost every page. All of this spiral bound between metal covers described alternately as innovative and aggressive or as good TV trays. Its famous Mylar wrapper made the book into a candy bar or a condom or a bottom: "We wanted," said Baron, "there to be an act of entering." Making *Sex* required three quarters of a million pounds of steel, a three-story printing press, and the assistance of at least one MacArthur Fellow. It was printed in a mere fifteen days.

*Sex* sold half a million copies within weeks of its release, making it a publishing event of unprecedented proportions, with another five hundred thousand copies put on sale simultaneously in Japan, Britain, France, and Germany. Sales and profit margins were said to be "astronomical" by any recognized industry or popular standard—certainly they were, even by comparison to two other titles which made trade news and hit the bestseller lists in November 1992: *The Autobiography of Malcolm X*, buoyed by expectations for the release of Spike Lee's film, shipped only three hundred thousand copies in the first half of 1992; and Warner's "instant" Clinton picture book, scheduled for release just after the election, had a first printing of just one hundred thousand copies.

At the same time, *Sex* made publishing history in a different way. Time-Warner, operating by the Madonnaesque erotics which holds that "the best way to seduce someone is by making yourself unavailable," deliberately limited the press run for *Sex*, printing far fewer copies than their prepublication hype had prepared a market for. (Here the widely circulated rumor of a plan for a cheaper and differently formatted version of the book—attributed to Warner Books president Larry Kirshbaum in *Publishers Weekly* but now denied by *Sex*'s publicists—is obviously of relevance.) Booksellers complained of receiving only partial shipments, and they, in turn, were often forced to limit the number of books a customer could buy. Review copies, distributed in advance to what one publicist called "select publications only," were simply not to be had by the time *Sex* arrived in stores. This constriction of supply and distribution was somewhat at odds with the "all access" mode of the book's contents and their prepublication dissemination—indeed, it was apparently at odds with the whole modus operandi and ethos of the Gone Platinum Blond phenomenon. It's still an open question whether manufactured scarcity of this kind is going to turn out to be the symptom of some new marketing philosophy at Time-Warner or elsewhere in the entertainment industry, but in this case it surely contributed to the noticeable "eventness" of the *Sex*-event in the sense that it produced, not only the usual body of consumers, but also a body of deliberately frustrated consumers.

This coming of the book-as-happening found media critics hurriedly transvaluing their usually unquestioned and comfortable assumptions about the criteria for assessing a book's importance (size of print run, advance advertising budget, newsworthiness, reputation of author, even sexiness); the enormity of *Sex*'s review-worthiness somehow rendered it a nonbook. "*Sex*," protested Giselle Benatar of *Entertainment Weekly* "is less a book than a slickly contrived, shrewdly marketed happening." Caryn James of the *New York Times* wrote: "To regard [*Sex*] as a book at all, to debate its merits as photography or erotica, is to play into the hands of Madonna's hype machine." Robert Hoffler of *Newsday* opined that "Pornography...doesn't hold up to serious analysis." (At the level of popular reception, a similar logic translated into *Sex*'s unreadability, as would-be collectors refused to cut open the Mylar packaging—rather ironically, perhaps, maintaining Madonna's virginal state.)

Flaunting its disrespect for the already flimsy boundaries between advertisement and editorial, publishing and reviewing,

y and merit, *Sex*-the-happening provoked critical ire. Its
 ̲ ̲ ̲ ̲ ̲ption was, however, different in kind from that of one of its
stablemates at Time-Warner: Ice-T's recording, "Cop Killer,"
which had also stirred angry emotions the previous summer.
*Newsweek* asked, "Will the pop diva's Mylar-bagged fantasy become another 'Cop Killer?' Not likely. While Ice-T's murderous
anthem provoked police boycotts and an uproar at the Time-
Warner annual shareholders' meeting, *Sex* seems less an abdi-
cation of public responsibility than a violation of taste." If
Madonna's *Sex* struck critics as being too staged, Ice-T's "Cop
Killer" seemed all too real; it elicited a "public" outcry which ultimately led to the removal of the track from Ice-T's album.
"Cop Killer" had proved *too* happening; Madonna's *Sex* was
destined to become a virtual non-event.

Yet despite obvious differences in the critical handling of
these two Time-Warner products, both "text-events" clearly
tested the limits of mainstream criticism which, in the end,
couldn't manage to treat either of them in quite the same way as
other cultural objects. In the case of *Sex*, the pre-packaged dollarwise diva was rebuked for her keen desire to conflate reception with production (or, to put it another way, her desire to
control reception by producing it—and here we might mention
that Madonna's most frequently remarked and reviled personality flaw is her need to control). Conversely, in the case of Ice-
T, the problem was Time-Warner's failure to package things
tightly enough. There the space between production and reception seemed too large; large enough, in fact, to abet—never
mind what Sister Souljah said about murderous lyrics being
mere fantasy—a riot or two.

Somewhere in the *terrain vague* between *Sex* and "Cop
Killer" lies this republic's comfort zone, where power and capital never ultimately determine thought but where, equally,
thought never seriously threatens power and capital. In this
arena, all the news that's fit to print is supposed to be produced
and circulated by an independent press which can neither be
bribed nor cowed. Attention to this zone has generally focused
upon limitations placed on the organs of free speech by the
state and, more specifically, upon those notoriously vexing legal

notions which regulate public speech. Most familiar here are cases and rulings concerned with obscenity ("we know it when we see it," or more lately, "what the ordinary man would find obscene using community standards of decency") or with "fighting words" (which allowed the courts, perhaps perceptively, to prohibit the distribution of socialist propaganda by likening it to screaming "Fire" in a packed theater). Everything from casebooks to civics lessons to *L.A. Law* leads us to believe that regulation of speech is by-and-large governmental and by-and-large regrettable; treasured tales of the First Amendment feature uncompromising reporters, tough-minded editors and the public-with-a-right-to-know, pitted against unscrupulous owners, craven politicos and secretive organizations. Neither Ice-T nor *Sex* was, however, officially repressed—the state as such made no serious threats to censor. Instead, these text-events seemed to test the limits of high-minded editors and responsible journalists who, in their routine reviewing and reporting capacities, carefully orchestrated "public" rejection notices. What we see, then, is the internalization of regulatory functions on the part of those same media whose very credibility relies upon their antagonism to regulation of speech. Accordingly, *Sex* and Ice-T are deemed excessive not because they are really obscene or inflammatory but because they may raise uncomfortable questions concerning the routine involvement (and routine disavowal) of power in the formation of "public" opinion. This is the literal scandal which the media continually disavow. Ventriloquizing for the outraged public that they allegedly represent and serve, the free speech professionals effectively protect their heavy investments in First Amendment mythography.

Given the jealousy with which this myth is guarded, Time-Warner president Larry Kirshbaum's fantasy of a review-proof book seems likely to remain fantasy. All publicity, they say, is good publicity. Just the same, it's unlikely that Time-Warner was really thrilled by the largely unthrilled response of the critics ("*Sex* is here! Was I shocked? No. Was I bored? Yes," wrote celebrity celebrity Liz Smith.) On the other hand, the way critics and journalists reacted, sleepily, to *Sex* made Steven Meisel's boast seem a very safe bet indeed: "I don't think anyone else needs to do another photo essay on erotica." Critical refusals to take *Sex* seriously might seem in retrospect like just a lover's spat, or perhaps a little game designed to spice up the relationship between huge corporate publishers and their tributary media. After the lengthy prepublication foreplay, the actual *Sex*-orgy, as hosted by Time-Warner and attended by the mostly bored media, was more like a quiet night in front of the telly—a bit anticlimactic. The publishing event of the century proved a non-eventful event, or an eventish non-event, attended by enormous noise, more enormous sales, and the widespread view that the most tasteful and decent response would be to say we should say nothing, or just say "So?"

## II. Only the one who takes away the pain can hurt you

*Madonnarama* arose from our very ordinary interest in the *Sex*-event. Like the Gulf War, the trial of William Kennedy Smith, the confirmation hearings of Clarence Thomas, and the debate about gays and lesbians in the military, *Sex* was the sort of public spectacle which, while commonplace in North American culture, is nonetheless produced as an extraordinary event, even as a crisis. By definition and design, crises are opportunities to rework ideological and cultural alignments; crises command public attention (public attention is commanded) precisely because they are the events by and in which relevant publics will (or will not) be reconstituted. Thus while the crisis endures, a variety of privatized institutions—the bus, the bar, the supermarket, the radio, the office—function as simulacra of public space. However cynical the invitation to think, however overdetermined the nature of our speech—we will talk.

But if our talk is the mark of crisis, it is also the sign that crisis management has begun; all talk looks forward to resolution and to the terms of a more or less satisfactory settlement, depending on your interest in exploiting the occasion. *Madonnarama* arose, too, from our disappointment in the provisional settlement over *Sex*. It wasn't so much a disappointment in *Sex* itself—though we both perhaps felt that the paraded banality of Madonna's sexual imaginings was more comical than provocative. Rather, our disappointment resided in the fact that the crisis surrounding the book was managed in terms which allowed for very little in the way of ideological realignment. There simply was not enough discussion about, let alone redeployment of, its crucial ingredients—sex, race, power and capital. This is not at all to imply that we thought Madonna herself ever intended to provoke any such revision; even proponents of *Sex* would have to admit that, once you've passed over the book's perfunctory waves in the direction of "sex-education" or AIDS-awareness, there's little between these spiral-bound pages that even hints at what you might call a *political* desire. But we did feel that some of the energy and capital invested in the book's production and reception could have been released in the service of something more widely significant, something less contained, something less stage-managed, something that might engage the layers of everyday life. So, we asked ourselves, what might have sufficed to turn this non-event into the occasion for a sustained crisis? Could it still be done?

Certainly not with ease. Standing in the way of, but crucially necessary to such a project are the same media that found Madonna's sexual self-exposure so quickly forgettable. Culture is, for better and worse, commodified; and publicity *is* a principle way for capitalism to produce information. Accepting that there can be no unmediated criticism, it remains true that commodification by and in the media poses special problems for public awareness and provocation. Chief amongst these might be the need to continually revolutionize the means of semiotic production—the need to make that most astonishingly modernist of cultural forms, the news. Doubtless (and symptomatically) it's boring to (re)remark upon the media's "forgetfulness" when it comes to issues of boring but ongoing relevance and importance (of which media forgetfulness is just one). Today (routine) domestic violence, (continued) racism in Germany, the (going nowhere) *intifada*, the (centuries old) struggles of Native Americans, or the (same old) Latin American debt crisis have all dropped from the headlines in favor of (new) gang violence,

(more) ethnic cleansing in Bosnia, (rising) Muslim fundamental-
ism, or (yet another revised) estimate of the deficit. But like all
affect and judgment, and like *Sex* itself, boredom and non-
newsworthiness are structured by relations of sex, power and
capital. If power only rarely forces or prohibits speech directly,
it is forever shaping its temporality and terms, forever struc-
turing relations of speech and silence. So it is to the minute
workings of speech production that we have to look to discern
the concrete workings of power as it inflects "response," sexual
or otherwise.

Thus the media's boredom can be seen as something more
than a mere swipe at Time-Warner for overstepping the bounds
of publishing decorum. *Sex* offered us an unusual opportunity
to examine the most basic terms of collective life—what else is
there besides sex, race, capital, and power? None of those terms
could really have gone unnoticed, so brazenly are they part of
*Sex* and the *Sex*-event; yet still the media yawned, occasionally
guffawed, and finally demurred, preferring a nap to a sensible
discussion of how, if at all, Madonna's crass self-proclamation
differs from business as usual. Pointing to Madonna's scan-
dalous flirtation with marginalized sexualities, the media de-
clared—as if they themselves had ever actually allowed us to
know this—that everything in *Sex* could be readily had at your
average newsstand and was therefore not worthy of comment.
Short of ignoring something all together—hardly a possibility
here, given the mutual investments of Time-Warner and those
who cover Time-Warner—to say that these things are not worth
comment is the most sweeping gesture of control that the media
have. As Nancy Neiman, the Warner Books executive who over-
saw the whole project, put it to *Entertainment Weekly* (a wholly
owned subsidiary of Time, Inc.): "Sex had the power to be explosive. That had to be managed." (She might have said the
same about "Cop Killer.")

*Madonnarama* assumes that *Sex could* have had the power
to be really explosive, and tries to find out whether and where
that power survives or can be reborn as a site of or resource for
thought and action. Michiko Kakutani's sneering *New York
Times* review of *The Madonna Connection*—a book which, like

this one, though from a more academic quarter and in more tex-
tualist terms, seeks to capitalize on Madonna's popularity—
provides a rough index of where and from whom future *Sex* talk
*won't* be welcomed. In a piece which seemed willfully to mis-
comprehend the project's very aims, writers who examined the
emerging relationship between academia and popular culture
industries were chastised for talking like fans; those who addressed the eternal return of certain issues—like appropriation,
feminism, postmodernism, race, sexuality, authenticity, capital—on the American cultural scene were dismissed for asking
nothing new. For those of us struggling to point out the relevance of those issues, and to problematize the media's arro-
gantly populist blockage, such a dismissal is flabbergastingly
apropos—it typifies the very problem in its disingenuousness.
Extended reflection on Madonna, or on popular culture in general, will inevitably attract the same criticisms as *Sex* itself:
this is "solipsistic," "pretentious blathering," whose authors
can only "huff and puff and create an enormous amount of hot
air" and who are—not to put too fine a point on it—far too the-
oretically minded and too heavily burdened with jargon. It
bothered Kakutani that so much capital and "years in graduate
school" should have been expended only to result in such "obvious assessments." Presumably it's because such assessments
are so staggeringly obvious that they rarely find their way into
the kind of low- to middle-brow rag for which Kakutani writes:
we've all seen race/class/gender, etc. before, and it's hardly the
business of real-life grownups to talk about it. "One cringes to
think what prepubescent wannabes will make of [*Sex*'s] relentless equation of sex and power," she says, implying that adults
who deign to notice the equation should say nothing about it.
Once again the tender sensibilities of the young and innocent
are invoked to remind us not to talk about such crude and im-
polite stuff.

From the point of view of the many adults who are, or
would be, or wannabe, interested precisely in making something of that equation, all of this shushing ought to appear
more repressive than anything so incidental as Madonna's alleged appropriation of subcultural signifiers. In much cultural

criticism, appropriation has been conceptualized within the matrix of identity politics; appropriation, more or less, means adopting the cultural codes of a group to which you don't "really" belong. This way of putting things begs the question, since the issue of whether or not the use of something not your own (assuming that deed and title are clear) can be called appropriation crucially depends on the terms of trade. Taking what isn't yours can be theft, but it can also be part of a fair and consensual exchange. Properly deployed, then, appropriation can point up existing injustices and chronic power imbalances. Understood that way, appropriation seems a feasible notion for exploring much more than just Madonna's relationship to the cultures she has come to inhabit and to exhibit. Appropriation would call attention, for instance, to the general media practice of *leasing* subcultural issues for just so long as the "general public" finds them interesting, and for no longer. Such a practice depends, of course, on uneven relations of power between the general public (unquestioningly constructed as straight—it won't always find sexual minorities of continual concern; constructed as nationalist—having only so much tolerance for foreign affairs; constructed as pro-business—the everyday workings of the bond market but not those of unions are its concern; and so on) and the special interests that are defined in relation to it. In Hannah Arendt's unsurpassed formulation, power is power to set the agenda. After that it doesn't matter so much *what* gets said. Those on the margins of the mainstream agenda scramble for a moment in the general spotlight, but as soon as those at the center have had their fill, all bets are off, all issues go back into the closet. Call it unrequited love.

The project of *Madonnarama* is, quite simply, to put some of those dismissed-as-boring issues back on the table. While there isn't any hope (or, indeed, intention) of countering Madonna's *Sex* (we couldn't possibly afford it—not the production values, not the advertising, and certainly not the state protection), what can be attempted is an exercise in enforcing or—less grandly and more realistically—*imagining* somewhat fairer terms of cultural trade. Perhaps what's imaginable here are the terms of what Andrew Ross calls "cultural justice." Such terms would grant those who have invested so much in Madonna, Time-Warner and the tributary media, the chance to see a return we can't usually expect: free speech on the topics of sex, power and capital, all pronounced a bit more loudly than is polite and a bit longer than is "interesting." Such terms would help to re-open those same old questions that have always had to be broached by those who can't afford it, who can't command media attention, but who nevertheless wish to investigate and transform the regimes of silence and quotidian invisibility to which so many are subject.

We're interested in what can perhaps be called an engagement with the media wherein Madonna is produced and where she works—an engagement that would help point towards some new sense of what sustained critique might actually look like, why currently it so often seems unsuccessful, why it's so vulnerable to being blocked by the media, why it's certainly always only partial, and why it often lands up being dismissed as simple gainsaying.

### III. If this commodity could speak, what would it say?

In soliciting essays for this collection, we thought first of writers whose responses we wanted to hear, writers whose involvement with popular culture has been sustained and thoughtful, or activists whose political work we support. Most contributors to *Madonnarama* are in one way or another on the left. Most would probably speak of themselves as gay or lesbian; they're certainly pro-lesbigay and sex-positive. Which isn't to say they're necessarily *Sex*-positive (some are, some aren't); rather, we might describe them as *Sex*ploitative, in that most of them want to *use* the book and *use* Madonna for the sake of the kind of engagement we've just described. Critical use of Madonna should perhaps be distinguished from the critical practice of recuperation. Rather than setting out to show that the Madonna text might be read into a progressive politics, contributors take it as axiomatic that texts will be intercepted in vested and purposeful ways. They go on from there to pick through and pick at points of acceptance and refusal, producing something like a map of allegiances and obstacles to affiliation.

One element, then, that links many of these authors is their frequent redeployment of *Sex*'s own prominent S/M (or "S & M," as Madonna writes) motif. Offered in *Sex* as not much more than a perverse practice on display for voyeuristic consumption, S/M can function for the writers in *Madonnarama* at once as an allegory for Madonna's relationship to her public and as a useful metaphor for their own reading and political practice. In this way most of the essays here both thematize and perform embraces and resistances—what Kirsten Lentz in her essay dubs kissing and hitting.

Writers often embrace Madonna's own tactics, attempting to control the signification of *Sex*. Susie Bright calls the book "by far her most serious work to date," and yet goes on to criticize it for not going far enough. Carol Queen attempts a sustained reading of *Sex* for its pleasure-producing possibilities, arguing that the book is in fact rather sexy if approached with the proper feminist and pro-sex attitude. Andrew Ross has an interestingly different way of contemplating *Sex*'s relation to feminism; his unwillingness to accept the shibboleths of liberal feminism allows him to explore race and class in ways that Queen does not. Readers will also detect the tactics of the parasite, the publicity hound, or the wannabe who capitalizes on public events. Pat Califia attempts to extend Madonna's working of S/M or even S/M-philia to despised or sometimes incarcerated fellow-practitioners. Cathay Che's loving effrontery acknowledges Madonna's support for her project, treating *Sex* itself much as Madonna treats her own collaborators.

Writers also insist on distinguishing their interests, needs, or communities from Madonna's. Douglas Crimp and Michael Warner complain that *Sex* is not queer enough; it would seem that queer is a constantly receding, even utopian category in their conversation—nothing existing will ever be queer enough—so theirs is not a claim for their identity against Madonna's appropriation. Rather it is a way of describing and measuring the ways Madonna and *Sex* might be usable. Even if at least one of them lands up expressing his boredom, neither is perhaps so appalled by the book as John Champagne who, in a similar project of describing and measuring, discovers the sadistic and homophobic elements in Madonna's power play. But even Champagne seems to demonstrate the hitting/kissing dialectic, and it appears again even in Simon Frith's review of Madonna's music. Frith's reactions to the *Erotica* CD often waver between a regard for the music and a problem with the attempts to make Madonna's voice sound erotic, which lead him to note that that struggle, internal to Madonna's recordings, leads not to good *Sex* but just to a good workout. Most unalloyed in her refusal of Madonna is bell hooks, whose only loyalty is to some of Madonna's previous incarnations, incarnations which are less touristic, less exoticist and less unmitigatedly racist.

Whatever the differences, ambivalences, points of negotiability and non-negotiability within the essays, in our view they all share the project of exploring or inventing the terms for talking back in a culture where talk's never cheap. What you won't find here is a collection of authentic expressivist voices—the voice of the black afrekete, the voice of queer boy, the lesbian intellectual, the black feminist—pronouncing the special interests of discrete identities. But what we hope you will find is something analogous to what Thomas Allen Harris collects here in his mini-documentary, where he attempts to reproduce the rhythms and varying registers of consumption ("humph, flip flip") and the tone of consumers' varying or even contradictory responses. *Madonnarama* attempts to represent and to shape a collective and contentious working out of lines of affiliation—not simply to Madonna and her function in a capitalist popular culture, but also to each other and to *our* function in a capitalist popular culture. It's only in that sense that when we speak about *Sex* we—like everyone else—might finally be able say more about ourselves than about Madonna.

Lisa Frank
Paul Smith
*March 1993*
*Pittsburgh*

CATHAY CHE

# Wannabe

*"On some level she's bored, and she has to do something to scare herself."* —Sandra Bernhard

*This way to the egress...*

**DISCLAIMER**

THIS PIECE IS ABOUT "DITA." DITA IS NOT MADONNA. MADONNA IS NOT DITA.

THIS PIECE IS ALSO ABOUT ME, AN AVERAGE WANNABE WITH AN OVERACTIVE IMAGINATION AND AN INSATIABLE DESIRE TO BLUR THE DISTINCTION BETWEEN LUST FOR AND IDENTIFICATION WITH MY SUBJECT. THE CONSTRUCTION OF THIS PIECE RECOGNIZES THE COMPLEX AND QUEER INTERPLAY OF BOTH PROCESSES AND RESISTS EMPLOYING GENDER AS A TOOL TO DIRECT MY EROS INTO PERMISSIBLE CATEGORIES.

A FAN MIGHT PAY HOMAGE TO A STAR BY CAMPING OUT ON THE SIDEWALK OUTSIDE HER NEW YORK APARTMENT, SCREAMING FOR HER ATTENTION. A WANNABE IS MORE LIKELY TO FOLLOW THE EXAMPLE OF THE ULTIMATE WANNABE HERSELF—MADONNA— AND TRY TO "BECOME." TO CARVE, STAMP, BURN, SHOCK, CONTRIVE, CONSTRUCT, SING, VIDEO, FILM, PHOTOGRAPH, AND/OR WRITE HER WAY INTO POPULAR DISCOURSE. MAYBE BY RESPECTFULLY BORROW

ING FROM OR MAKING REFERENCE TO ESTABLISHED
ICONS (TOO MANY TO NAME) WITH LUST, HUMOR AND
A CERTAIN IRREVERENCE. ALL THIS WITHOUT LOSING
A FOCUS ON HERSELF AND HER INTENT TO EXPAND
HER HORIZONS AND PUSH HER OWN LIMITS.

FANTASIES CAN BE THE SITE OF RESISTANCE. WHAT
FOLLOWS ARE FANTASIES I HAVE DREAMED UP. LIKE
MOST HUMAN BEINGS, WHEN I LET MY MIND WAN-
DER, I LET MYSELF GO. BUT MY FANTASIES TAKE
PLACE IN AN IMPERFECT WORLD. A WORLD WHERE
RACIAL AND SEXUAL STEREOTYPES COMPLICATE ANY
STRUGGLE FOR SEXUAL IDENTITY AND FREEDOM OF
EXPRESSION. A WORLD WHERE YOUNG ASIAN AMERI-
CAN WOMEN GROW UP SURROUNDED BY "TROUBLED"
ROLE MODELS. IN FACT A QUICK SURVEY OF THE MOST
VISIBLE ASIAN WOMEN IN AMERICA PRODUCES:

1) SOON-YI PREVIN—THE ADOPTED DAUGHTER OF AC-
TRESS MIA FARROW, WHO ALLEGEDLY "BETRAYED"
HER CHARITABLE MOTHER BY HAVING AN ILLICIT AF-
FAIR WITH MIA'S HUSBAND, WOODY ALLEN, A MAN 31
YEARS HER SENIOR.

2) CONNIE CHUNG—THE MEGA-SUCCESSFUL NEWS AN-
CHOR WHO HAD COSMETIC SURGERY TO HAVE HER
EYES LOOK "BIGGER" AND WHOSE ALLEGED PERSONAL
TRAGEDY IS HER INFERTILITY AND INABILITY TO
HAVE A BABY WITH HER INFAMOUS HUSBAND, TALK
SHOW HOST MAURY POVICH.

3) TINA CHOW—THE RICH AND BEAUTIFUL EURASIAN
MODEL AND FASHION ICON, NOW MARTYRED AS AN
ALLEGEDLY SEXUALLY "CHASTE" WOMAN WHO CON-
TRACTED THE HIV VIRUS DURING A BRIEF AFFAIR
WITH A BISEXUAL MAN. SHE IS NOW REMEMBERED AS
THE FIRST/ONLY FAMOUS WOMAN TO HAVE DIED OF
AIDS.

AND **4)** YOKO ONO—THE ARTIST WHO ALLEGEDLY MANAGED TO "CATCH" EX-BEATLE JOHN LENNON AND HOLD HIM IN A SEXUALLY PASSIONATE MARRIAGE UNTIL HIS DEATH BY ASSASSINATION. INFAMOUS FOR THE " HONEYMOON" WEEK SHE AND LENNON SPENT IN BED, ALLOWING THE PRESS TO PHOTOGRAPH THEM NAKED.

SO, UNFORTUNATELY AND UNSURPRISINGLY, NAGGING QUESTIONS ABOUT HOW REPRESENTATIONS OF ASIAN WOMEN'S SEXUALITY IN THE MEDIA AFFECT THE WAY I AM PERCEIVED SEXUALLY RUDELY INTRUDE, EVEN IN MY OWN FANTASIES.

STILL, IT IS MY INTENTION TO REMAIN MILITANTLY SEX-POSITIVE.

EVERYTHING YOU ARE ABOUT TO READ IS FICTIONAL. BUT IN GENERAL, WHEN I HAVE THE OPPORTUNITY TO MAKE MY FANTASIES REAL, I DO. AND I'M FULLY COMMITTED TO THE USE OF LATEX, EVEN THOUGH THE LUBE ON SOME CONDOMS SEEMS TOXIC, AND THE POWDER ON DAMS, GLOVES AND FINGER COTS GET WET AND ROLLS OFF IN LITTLE IRRITATING DOUGHLIKE BITS.

AND BY THE WAY, ANY SIMILARITY BETWEEN CHARACTERS AND EVENTS DEPICTED IN THIS PIECE AND REAL PERSONS AND EVENTS IS NOT ONLY INTENTIONAL, BUT RIDICULOUS. NOTHING IN THIS PIECE IS TRUE. I MADE IT ALL UP BECAUSE I THINK MADONNA'S BOOK *SEX* IS MEANT TO BE READ AND READ (IN)TO EVERY GAZER'S HEART'S CONTENT.

Hi Dita            Dolphin & Swan Hotel
                        Disney World

   Me and Sandy are lying topless by the
"lake" as middle-America looks on disapprovingly.
By the way, if this place isn't listed as a
seperate World Power yet, it should be. But
really, I'm lovin' it cause Sandy is here
and we both keep ~~busy~~ busting up over all
the icky-sticky family vacation memories
this place brings up. Remembering too much
can make us a little cranky, but then
we'll act "sexually inappropriate" or fuck
on some boat ride and feel lots better.
   Sandy is pretty fucking righteous—
what a world view. I love being next to
her, I love getting inside her. Hard to
imagine that just a month ago I was
desperately trying to get her attention by
throwing dried cranberries into her cleavage
from across a buffet table.
   You, of course, are a bond between
us. I don't know for sure how much of
her interest in me is motivated by unresolved feelings she has about you. And
I'm not going to bring up the subject because,
hell, I don't know exactly what my
motivations are either. Sandy's lips are a
major distraction / attraction for me, so BYE-
we're going to freak.
   As usual, I won't be sorry to return

to NYC. Afterall, I need my regular
dose of you. In fact I miss you and
want you so bad, it's almost like I've
never known you, pussy-love.

Yours Truly
XX Cathay X

P.S. How is the lovely Ingrid?

New York

Dear Dita,

Things have not been the same since you left. Of course, Sandy's back in LA now too. I just sit up at night with "The Robyn Byrd Show" laughing my head off at all the mock-sexy people. If Robyn ever stops weaving that macramé bikini, those pink cowboy boots and that heart pendant on her leather dog-collar, I will be seriously disoriented.

Afterwards, watching all those 970-geisha-To-Go "Oriental Outcall" ads really make my eyes glaze over. Asian women are such a popular fetish — right up there with S/M and Golden Showers. Too bad it's about a thousand percent more airtime than we get anywhere else on TV. I think this is haunting me.

Needless to say, I'm feeling kinda agitated and thus, I've done some great guerilla art posters that the crew and I have wheat-pasted all over the city. They are a big hit — Billy Norwich even mentioned them in his column. And I got this idea for a film — "wheat-pasters of the midnight Hour", a documentary about the people who put up the posters and the people who tear them down. We could even attempt some "cinema verite", and stage a confrontation!

You know, I had a dream about you, Sandy, Ingrid and me. We were all tormenting each other by saying nasty things about each other in interviews. Then we all looked so bad, we called a truce and signed with the same publicist. Then, we all sat at the same table with kd lang at the Grammy dinner. I think this symbolizes that I want to eat out with all of you together.

Anyway, can't wait until this weekend at your ~~place~~ place pussy-o!

Love XX
Cathay

Dear Dita,          New York

    Sandy's birthday is coming up and I want to plan a party. I can't decide between something public for the media to devour, or something small and intimate. It would be great to play out some sexual fantasy for her, something from Jacqueline Suzanne's Valley of the Dolls, but she's pretty much lived it all. She might like it if a woman jumped out of a cake. Since you seemed to get along last time, might you perform? And could you please bring Ingrid — I think she's finally starting to warm-up to me. Sandy is totally over her you know — her name has never come up. But then again, Sandy's obsessed at the moment. She's working on this BIG deal for her to star in some re-make Barbra Streisand musical. I hope the project pans out cause it seems to mean the world to her.

    And how are you pussy-mine? You've been kinda quiet lately. I heard you were in town a few days last week and didn't even call me. Trouble in paradise? Is it someone new — a man?

    I got some dick myself recently, a cute-butt waiter at Florent. People seem scandalized. Am I bisexual? I don't think so. Afterall, I'm not interested in men unless they'll turn over and let me fuck them, too. Though some of them are damn beautiful and I do fantasize about them. But you of course know what I mean.

I dis/miss your loving punishments even though I make myself come all the time thinking about them.

Love,
LaCathay XX

Dear Dita,                              New York

    Sandy's in town but I'm watching Robin Byrd alone - can you believe it? I'm mad at her. First she shows up with her faabulous fag friends at Cafe Tabac, and then drags us all to the most dreadful film — "Body of Evidence".

    As you've probably heard there is not one redeeming bit. At first it seemed to be making a point that just because a woman is into kinky sex, it doesn't mean she's evil. But of course, it turns out she is, and worse than that, she gets punished for it- literally blown away in the usual ugly brutal manner. Just another film feeding straight men's paranoia and fear of sexual women. And Sandy and her crew wouldn't walk out!

    You know, last week I killed some time watching "The Lover", "Damage" & "Indochine", and I just couldn't get turned on. The women and all the Asian people were all so tragic, I laughed until I cried. Definately more neurotic than erotic. Oh, where-oh-where are all the dirty movies I can relate to? Sometimes there's really nothing I want more... So here I am not picking-up the phone and Sandy's called about a dozen times. Only 5 days until her birthday gala- she better make it up to me quick! (sigh...)

    By the way, thanks for giving me Ingrid's # here - we're having lunch tommorow! Can't wait to see you Pussy-rub! Cathay

Dear Dita,                                    Five Island

   You were here for such a short time we really didn't get to do it enough! Don't stay in LA too long — it's not good for you and there's too much to miss in NYC. But you have Ingrid at your beck and call don't you, so even LA can be a little bit of heaven.

   Wasn't Sandy's party a scene? Gossip columnists will feed off it for months! The 2 of you on stage together was like a session with those drag queens The Dueling Bankheads. Bitter beauties — very amusing. And ~~its~~ I'm glad no one got hurt.

   When those supermodels jumped out of the cake with their wigs aflame! I've never screamed so much in my life! It's a good thing no eyebrows are "in" at the moment. After I put out that fire, you and Sandy were relatively easy. But it's obvious to everyone that if you could both just leave it alone, it would really be over.

   You and Sandy both get more and more fuck-able as you get older. So what if you had on the same Dior black demi-cup bras — you both have the best taste. And who gives a shit who has the bigger dick — Ingrid and I don't care as long as we get to kiss and smear both of your lipsticks in public.

   You both fuck like such real women that I am endlessly inspired by your pussy-joy, my pussy-joy. I saw a gay male porn flick the other day and took in a few new things I think we should try out. Miss you something awful — hurry back!
                 Your devoted fan, Cathay XX

Rita,                                    New York

    I'm still feeling a little raw, but
I wanted to write to let you know that
I know, and I see. I see it all now
that the lights are on.

    I guess I was blinded by lust.
Or maybe I was drugged up on fucking.
So your interest in my relationship
with Sandy was motivated by your
unresolved feelings about her. But it's
still shocking to me that you would
go so far as to sign a contract
to star in that god-damned Streisand
re-make yourself — are you crazy?!

    Needless to say Sandy was a
mess when she first found out, but
now she's just MAD at you and at
me. Of course she thinks I helped
you somehow — right, like I have
that kind of power and influence.
Not to say you ruined my relationship w/ Sandy. Sexually, I don't
think I was ever her thang — not
ethnic enough? or maybe too ethnic?
But don't get me started on this
subject.

    Oh, and Ingrid also told me
that ~~you~~ both you and Sandy
referred to me as "your precious

Japanese love-doll". Well! "Your precious love-doll" maybe, but how dare you throw in that "oriental" reference for dramatic effect — how dare you sexualize me through my ethnicity, or link my sexuality and ethnicity like some cheap over-saturated ~~stereotype~~ stereotype! You thought I was mad when you said you had "japanitis" in that documentary you made about you. And are you laughing at my anger?! I think I'm gonna be ~~sick~~ sick.

    I guess it's not news to you that Ingrid and I are hanging out together. You wouldn't be surprised at what a first generation Cuban and a third-generation Asian American can get up to. And I'm so satisfied that no pain or ~~punishment~~ seems to last. No illusions either.

    So next time you want pussy this good, let me know. I'd be happy to send you a dirty movie. A dirty movie of me and Ingrid ~~fucking~~.

        Gone,
          Cathay

## ACKNOWLEDGMENTS

I WOULD LIKE TO THANK EVERYONE IN ADDITION TO
MADONNA WHO MADE THIS PIECE POSSIBLE. SANDRA
BERNHARD FOR HER LIPS, THE BEGINNING AND END
OF MY CURRENT ORAL FIXATION. INGRID CASSARAS
FOR STATING THAT HER FAVORITE MOVIE OF 1993
WAS *BODY OF EVIDENCE*. RUTH WILSON GILMORE FOR
PLANTING THE SEEDS OF AN EDUCATION THAT JUST
WON'T QUIT. CHRIS TEEN & TRASH FOR SHOWING ME
THAT GENDER IS THE ULTIMATE SEX TOY. DIANE
TORR FOR BEING A CULTURALLY AUTHENTIC MALE
IMPERSONATOR, AND DEFYING IT ALL HER WAY.
GAYSHA, DAISY, MONA FOOT, EBONY JET, AFRO-DITE,
AND THE CONNIE GIRL AND OTHER YOUNG DRAG
QUEENS, KINGS AND TRANSSEXUALS OF COLOR WHO
HAVE HIT ME LIKE A TRUCK AND TAUGHT ME HOW TO
GENDER-FUCK. JOHN PALOMINO FOR GETTING RID OF
MY EYEBROWS ONCE AND FOR ALL. ASIANS EVERY-
WHERE WHO HAVE DARED TO BRING ATTENTION TO
THEMSELVES AND CONTINUE TO NOT BE AFRAID. GE-
NIUS! PERFECTION!

*Pussy rules the world...*

**thomas allen harris**

# phallic momma sell my pussy make a dollar

*The erotic is a resource within
each of us that lies in a deeply
female and spiritual plane, firmly
rooted in the power of our
unexpressed or unrecognized
feeling...*
—Audre Lorde

*Out of the blackest part of my soul,
across the zebra striping of my
mind, surges this desire to be
suddenly*
white.
—Franz Fanon

*November 22*
i am a black afrekete queen with medium-length
locks, a big round ass and cute titties. next to
me sits my blond ambition, a cute german with
silky blond hair from the top of his head to the
tip of his toes. bring me the scissors hans, I tell
him, smacking his backside as he gets up.

madonna's blond ambition. let's see what miss
thing is serving today.

hans returns to my side holding out the scissors
in both hands. thank you, i say giving him a

smile which warms his heart. i'm about to stab
into this package that i know contains
madonna's sex, but inspecting it again, i decide
against the scissors. laying them down, i begin
tearing away at the tape until one flap is free
only to reveal more tape. tear, rip open the
central compartment.

this could be a performance piece i say to hans
kneeling quietly beside me. of course he says,
and you're doing fine. i smile down at him
stroking the smooth hair on his head then
moving my hand down his hairy neck beyond
the collar to the rougher darker hairs on his
shoulders and back. he beams up at me. i know
i am i say.

i've reached a point where i can no longer
penetrate the packaging with my hands so I
retrieve the scissors. snip, cut and then open to
the inside and out springs madonna in silver,
mouth open, long dark lids, lashes and frosty
hair.

look! i say. it's madonna.

who sent you that? says hans, frowning. who
sent you that? he repeats.

this is too much i say looking at madonna then
back at hans who has moved behind me. two
blond ambitions and one black beauty. Creating
a nice neat inside-out oreo cookie. special on the
inside. of course.

don't open it says hans. it's boring.

how shall i open it? i say flipping the silver

colored plastic container over to inspect the
other side.

don't open it. it's boring.

shall I cut across her face hans, I ask.

don't open it he responds. i take the scissors
and cut across the top lid. black out.

daddy first introduced me to madonna years
ago—playing her record—she's a material girl
living in a material world—the one time i visited
him during four miserable years at harvard. of
course this was before he started leaving
messages on my answering machine calling me
and my lover at the time, you and that bitch you
living with—both bitches. mother fucking
bitches.

back on the sofa, sitting next to hans, i think:
judging from the way madonna presents herself,
we both had fantasies of growing up to be
marilyn as little girls and boys. but then, that
was before we knew any better.

*December 16*
mommy drops by to visit. this makes me very
happy—at least that's what i tell myself. first i
show her the catalogue for the meditation
retreat i plan to take next week. she reads it
through. then i show her madonna's sex. what
do you think? i ask. she opens it and flips
through. flip. very tired. flip. flip. it's really not
worth writing about. flip. i tell her: ma, they're
paying me a couple hundred dollars and I need
the money. well she says, perhaps. flip. if it
doesn't take too much time. flip. flip.

she flips a few more pages. the writing is more
transgressive than the pictures she says. flip. i
don't know that much about photography but
everything in here has been done before. flip.
flip. did you do it mommy? i wonder. do you
know about this first hand? i think. but i nod
my head in agreement. you're right i say.

this is trash she says. flip. nothing enticing or
shocking or beautiful. flip. flip. i'm trying to find
out what it's supposed to do. do? do! doo doo.

*December 17*
dinner with mother goes well and i go to see my
therapist, mr. x, the next day. at the end of the
session we are both sitting on the couch and i
am showing him how my mother casually
strokes me as we talk. i can tell he is getting
nervous and i am enjoying using borrowed
tricks from mother. i finally release his hand. i
reach in my black bag, pull out madonna's sex
and tell him look at it.

flip. flip. humph flip. humph. is this a limited
edition? he asks. flip. is it the same as the hard
cover in the stores? humph. flip. what do you
think? i ask. nicer to see them in this large
format he responds adding a humph on the next
flip.

well, she really looks good these days.
large...production...value.

lots of talk in the therapeutic community about
who she is and what she represents. flip.
psychologically speaking she would be called a
phallic narcissist. flip. a classic phallic female.
flip. flip. I haven't followed her that closely. flip.

I don't like her music. I didn't see truth or dare
where did you get this special edition by the
way? flip. flip. flip. flip.

i push him for more as he scans the pages of
madonna's sex: she takes sex as a recreational
activity. flip. a sort of female version of the don
juan character. flip. the question is how much of
this is her public persona and how much is a
reflection of what's going on behind the scenes.
flip. flip. but either way he adds. flip. she
wouldn't put herself in this position unless
there was something in her background that
makes this type of public exhibition fulfilling.
flip. flip. flip. he closes the book.

just before i leave his office he confides: her
public persona is so strong, so embedded, that
therapy would be difficult if not impossible
because the minute anything began to crumble,
the public persona would come up like a steel
wall that's bigger than life.

*December 19*
a few nights later i meet my friend xuana, a
filmmaker who is going to edit my film ALL IN
THE FAMILY, a feature-length project which
looks at black families through the eyes of black
lesbian and gay siblings. at dean street café in
brooklyn, we have wicked ale and blackened
vodoo beer, deep fried stuffed clams and fried
calamari with red tomato salsa sauce.

i take out sex knowing that there is a high
probability it is going to get greasy and stained.
xuana: ohhhh thomas, i've heard so much about
this she says wiping her hands and pushing
back the food. not too much good though. flip.

but what I'm seeing flip flip i like. flip. great
packaging. look at this shit. serious dykes. flip.
where did you get it baby? flip. do you think i
should re-do my blond streaks and tips? flip.
flip. my roots are growing in but it's so
pretentious. flip.

this guy's face is great. flip. flip. flip. what do
you think about my hair? flip. i've heard so
many terrible things and i hate her. flip. you're
not listening to me! what do you think of it? i'm
such an easy sell. flip. flip. isabella is so wild
she doesn't care. flip. madonna makes me sick
though but i like it. flip. flip. flip. what are you
doing thomas. writing this down. you're terrible.
flip.

flip. she wrote that! i think we've all done that.
when I was eighteen my second boyfriend made
me taste myself. flip.

flip. flip. to the black shots—bdk for big daddy
kane and mn for miss naomi. i'm sick of
madonna. i'm absolutely outraged. trashy white
girl. flip. flip. look at naomi. look at her. she's
too game. she don't need that. she's too fierce for
that. flip. flip. and flip.

I think i'll buy a couple of these for x-mas
presents says xuana closing the book and
looking at the back cover.

*December 20*
hans returns to hamburg just a few days before
karl arrives from berlin. karl and i are friends.
he saved my life in berlin and fell in love but i
wanted no part of that. only friendship and sex
please. he has a nice tight body and muscles

that are long, lean, hard and prickly—especially
on his chest and stomach where he shaves down
the dark blond spikes. his nose is long—almost
as long as the penis of my last boyfriend. i
fantasize about—well, i mean i'm looking
forward to wild passionate sex that doesn't stop
moving in between soft and hard lifting me off
the ground bucking on a big white...

karl arrives with tales of new boyfriend drama
and refuses to have sex with me. mind you we
kiss, sleep together naked, hug constantly and
sit on each other's laps. lying in bed he tells me:
because of my feelings for my [new] boyfriend i
can only give you my body, not my soul and
thomas this would not feel very nice for me. i
respect this and ask him to help me jerk off.

it is very clinical. we won't be doing that again.

*December 28*
karl returns from chicago where he was visiting
his new boyfriend also black with a big round
ass and cute tits.

i pull out madonna's sex sometime during karl's
three-week stay. very interesting that she uses
this metal cover he says, because the project is
exciting but cold. no fun he says. flip. flip. big
daddy doesn't look like he's having much fun
either. flip. i mean he really looks like: when am
i going to get paid for this shit. flip.

*December 29*
my cousin malika comes over to borrow some
food. I give her the two cold roasted potatoes
wrapped in foil. what's this she says pointing
then reaching for madonna's sex. she opens the

book flip flip. crazy bitch! flip. do you have a lot of
violent sexual fantasies? flip. she's definitely a
survivor, an incest survivor. flip. it may even be
her father. flip. but then this could just be a
marketing ploy. flip. is this what's really going on
with her? flip. rather than dealing with the pain
she is glamorizing it.

flip. flip. i read that in the contract they told her
no penetration, no children, no animals and she
said sex with the young can be fun. flip. i have a
problem with that. flip. did you see truth or
dare? flip. i think she has stuff with her father.
flip. flip. i have to ask you a question tommy,
she says looking up at me. what are crabs? flip.

is that pee going in his mouth? flip. it's not that
i think this book is tired, i just think she's
unconnected. flip. oh they do have animals. she's
got a deer eating her—or maybe it's a rabbit.
what is that? flip.

she's heavy into power too. "when he comes i
want to see the moment of surrender." flip.
misogyny that's when men hate women. what's
the word for women who hate men. i get that
from her. flip.

hum, she started masturbating late. flip. i was
three when i started. but it could have been
from the sexual abuse in my nursery school.
actually the more i think about it the more it
was...

*December 30*
xuana drops by to give me x-mas presents—two
fabu cassettes—she doesn't remember i have a
cd. an hour later my date aaron arrives ready to

give me my once-a-year chocolate treat to feed
my sweet tooth. xuana feels like she's in the way
so she picks up madonna's sex which is lying on
the table and looks at it for a few moments. flip.
flip. madonna is like a predatory animal she
says between flips.

xuana is waiting for another friend, the famous
black lesbian filmmaker, to pick her up. when
she arrives she spots madonna's sex on the
table. wow! she says opening the book seeing
another famous-lesbian-club-diva-artist-activist
acquaintance named julie with her lips pressed
against madonna's left nipple. she got to be
with madonna!!! flip.

they finally leave and me and aaron get into the
kitchen and start cooking a double layered
chocolate custard cream pie.

*January 5*
i visited my friend la tina, a playwright. brought
along sex cause i know she can read fast and
furiously: oh this is sex. flip. and there she is.
flip. did you buy this? I was going to say,
thomas I know you have more sense than to pay
money for this. flip. flip. she just can't get
enough of herself can she. flip. flip. flip.

ow! a knife! flip. I wonder what her real purpose
in doing this was. flip. great photographs. I
wonder what's next for her. x-rays of her next
cervix exam? flip. close up of madonna's vulva,
live on regis and cathy lee. flip.

mapplethorpe did not get this much attention.
but then he wasn't blond and his models
weren't blond. flip. flip. but it said a lot more.

(aside: she's got a great body.) mapplethorpe
had more artistic importance in documenting
sexual lifestyles.

flip. i don't know what this means. why do we
want to see this? flip. what is it with her? flip.
why does she want us to see her fingering
herself? flip. flip.

oh. it's big daddy. flip. do we get to see what he
has in his pants? flip. flip. flip. that's it on the
black people?! back track flip. she could have
some more black people in here for me. flip.

she has a deep need to expose herself for
reasons that are not that clear. flip. the problem
is this book has no gravity. flip. she's going
overboard with her self assertion. she's
asserting herself in a masculine way for every
woman. flip. which is why i like her. flip. but i
think she's lost her femininity and become too
butch—not in the literal but in a figurative
way—dominating just like men. flip. instead of
developing a female sensibility. because look
she says flipping from one photo to another and
reading the text—these are all male fantasies
played out by a woman. flip flip. double flip. flip.

honey if you're going to do it, then max it out.
do it in such a way as to say this is some girl
shit. but this masculine, mannish thing is
nowhere near as interesting as if she had some
female thing going on. flip flip. yeah. yeah you're
taking power and shoving it down a man's
throat but for whose pleasure? that's what i
want to know. flip. this book is about having a
penis but i wish she had a big pussy in her head

and worked that. flip. but see pussy is not quite
as marketable. flip. and that's the sad thing
because if anybody could make a female erotic
agenda available it would be her. la tina hands
sex back to me saying:

my final word is: miss thing has a big dick in
her brain and it's too bad she doesn't have a big
clitoris there instead.

*January 20*
three weeks after the deadline for this fucking
piece on madonna's sex. let's see what i can
write without opening up the book.
titillating...without any real newness. initially, i
thought the images had the potential to enlarge
the mainstream economy of—no. this sounds
too academic. let's see. the images would open
people's minds—but i reflect on the fact that
many minds are already open in this direction. i
personally don't strive for the power of
madonna's sex. as a man who is involved in
healing, nurturing, real communication that
builds towards positive change, healing change,
this book blah blah blah blah blah.

i am frustrated. karl has been here for almost
three weeks and the most we do is hug and kiss
and make goo goo eyes at each other over the
safety of a restaurant table. as he says we give
each other much tenderness kisses. but i'm a
horny bitch who wants some dick. my new
year's resolution was abstinence to change the
flow of my energy. but i decide i've had enough.
and i don't want to drive to the bijou to get my
rocks off. in fact, i don't want to leave my house
at all. so i decide to take a little peek at

madonna's book for the first time alone with no
one else around. jar of vaseline in place, open
and dipped. flip. flip. flip.

uh uh. big letdown literally and figuratively. the
book is dry. so i close her, then close my eyes.
take a deep breathe and go for it honey.


*Thanks to all participating friends and family.*

ANDREW ROSS

# This Bridge Called My Pussy

To begin with the obvious, the least queer people to occupy the pages of *Sex* are Vanilla Ice and Big Daddy Kane. The sequences in which they appear are abject studies in heterosexual discomfort. Ice, the hypester from hell, so desperately wants to be seen there but can't generate any heat. He seems to be the one person who doesn't know he's only been invited along for his kitsch value as a has-been who really never was in the first place. By contrast, Kane, the strong, silent ladies' man, would clearly rather be somewhere else. Neither seems to know where to put his hands; the only safe place is between the lady's legs. Not that Madonna could care less. Sexual diversity, after all, is her semi-encyclopedic aim—all access, straights included somewhere—and so the end justifies the means, even if it never justifies her love of access. Perhaps it might have made a difference if she had chosen, say, a bubbly manchild like Marky Mark, or a lecherous prankster like Sir Mix-A-Lot, but the joke would still have been on them. And why not? It's hard to argue with a world where straight masculinity's most powerful genre is that of farce, which mixes self-ridicule with good sportsmanship, rather than tragedy, which involves the daily (social) death of others. Apart from the rape scene in the school gym, where the unlikely assailants are nipple-ringed refugees from central casting at the Vault (a camp echo of the lesbian slave sequence, where torturers hold a knife to her crotch), Madonna's *Sex* is a world which the unqueer, unlike the undead, do not haunt with menace, and where picaresque adventures in the flesh trade are conducted with safe passage across a landscape lavished with neon proclaiming "This Is Dangerous. Try It," and, more subliminally, "Goods Non-Returnable." It's a playground that might be an obstacle course if you're not in the mood for a lesson ("things can go really wrong"), but if you are, then you might think it's the sentimental education of someone else's lifetime; the mind fuck of the century, the sassiest way yet of going down on history. Smells Like Queer Spirit. (Which Madonna could seriously bottle and market, if only Warner were in the perfume business).

It's all the more important to recall, then, that Ice and Kane are rappers—this is no coincidence—and, as such, they are *Sex's* dubious ambassadors from another theater of the cultural wars, where queerness is a big-time liability and not a raidable asset for the Time-Warner-Madonna Complex. In the theater called rap, especially hardcore, hands are what you put your life in, so you'd better know what to do with them, or else keep 'em to yourself. "Smooth—not what I am/Rough—cause I'm a man," sing the dire straights. "No Vaseline" goes the chorus line. Gotsa to be hard. Or Boom Bye Bye, in the words of Buju Banton's battyboy bashing anthem of Jamaican dancehall, gangsta rap's fellow traveler in the killing fields of homophobia. This is the other leading edge of popular culture, not the one that teaches the Big Gender Fuck, but the one which preaches Big Fucking Gender. Of course, it's conventional by now to say that both are striking a pose—the hand that squeezes the trigger in the Hip Hop Nation and the clamp that squeezes the nipple in the Queer Nation. It's conventional to say that both are harmless, fantasmatic representations, with no effectivity in the real world...blah, blah, blah. It's even conventional to say that the utopian conventions of Madonna's "It makes no difference if you're black or you're white/If you're a boy or a girl" are as conventional as the dystopian conventions of Ice-T's spoken intro to "Body Count":

> You know sometimes I sit at home you know and I watch TV, and I wonder what it would be like to live someplace like, you know, the Cosby Show or Ozzie and Harriet, where cops come and got your cat out of the tree, and all your friends died of old age. But, you see, I live in South Central Los Angeles, and, unfortunately, shit ain't like that. It's real fucked up.

Remember, however, that, in both cases, we are still talking about culture created around places where death is a familiar visitor—the bodybag legacies, respectively, of the driveby or the killercop, and the AIDS hospice bed or the queerbasher. Whether utopian or dystopian, these are stories about wishing that the daily world were propelled by the power of possibility, and not by the channeling of the death drive by the powers that be. But the difference between them, as everyone ought to know, lies in the divergent careers of Ice-T and Madonna at Time-Warner. In 1992, the rapper's decision to "voluntarily" withdraw "Cop Killer" from the *Body Count* CD set the standard for widespread music industry censorship, at the same time as it caved in to police and right-wing pressure groups. Madonna's decision to suck toes and bite asses in public set a new standard for celebrity exhibitionism, at the same time as it profitably exploited outrage from the moralistas. Time-Warner executives, in the meantime, kept their noses clean. To begin with, they turned the *Body Count* affair into a free speech platform for the corporation. Co-CEO Gerald Levin publicly proclaimed that the censorship of "Cop Killer" "would be a signal to all artists and journalists that if they wish to be heard, they must tailor their minds and souls to the reigning orthodoxies." As the pressure built, from the White House down, there was every indication that Warner began discretely to put the rapper's back to the wall while publicly maintaining an anti-censorship stance. No one who smelled the post-L.A. fear of white America in May and June of 1992 would fully believe Ice-T's claim that he had not been coerced into his decision. By contrast, Warner welcomed *Sex* in November as the messianic harbinger of a nirvanic phase of development within the culture industries. In the words of Warner Books president, Laurence Kirshbaum, *Sex* was a "review-proof" publication, pushing this Warner product into the realm of the guaranteed sell, beyond all critical influence, beyond the vagaries of reception. Free at last, the Industry Transcendent. Or, alternately, the hand that gave us Madonna was the hand that eventually took away *Body Count* in February 1993 when Ice-T was finally released from his Warner contract for "creative differences."

Even though Madonna is not actually gay, and "Cop Killer" was being aired circa the tragedy of South-Central L.A., there was an overriding pattern here, for which the differing treatment of each product was quite symptomatic. Madonna, for example, was able to mobilize key sectors of the FBI in a sting that tracked down some pre-publication prints stolen from Lexington Labs: "Thanks," she cites in *Sex's* acknowledgments, "to Gavin De Becker and the FBI for rescuing photographs that would make J. Edgar Hoover roll over." (Given the recent revelations about photographs of Hoover himself, this is a rich comment.) In the meantime, the sons of J. Edgar were probably routinely wiretapping Ice-T and his posse. Whenever Ice-T performs in public, he summons up the ghosts of Malcolm and Martin by openly predicting, for his audience, the day of his own martyrdom while offering some conclusive wisdom: never bow down before a badge, and take care, there are criminals in uniforms out there on the streets.

However apparent the double standard, I don't want to suggest that the different careers of Madonna and Ice-T at Warner can *entirely* be ascribed to discriminatory differences in the way in which sex and race are treated within the culture industries. Madonna has had her own run-ins with the forces of censorship, and the public demonizing of any gangsta rapper can hardly be considered a career setback. Besides, in 1992, the outlawing of Ice-T, however self-generated, took place against the backdrop of the much discussed commodification of Malcolm X. Madonna's queer-positive book appeared against the backdrop of an emergent wave of anti-gay sentiment. Don't be confused. These are the contradictory outcomes of pursuing a politics of race and a politics of sex in a consumer culture.

By the time that the Mylar-wrapped *Sex* shot to the top of the bestseller lists in post-election November (usurping right-wing humorist Rush Limbaugh's ominously titled *The Way Things Ought To Be* for a few brief weeks only), some optimists were all too ready to see its relatively yawn-filled reception as proof that the cultural wars were now over. A low- to mid-intensity conflict throughout the eighties (when many non-paranoids suspected that Margaret Atwood's *The Handmaid's Tale* might be more like prophecy than SF), these wars had reached drum fever pitch only months before, when zealot hacks at the Republican Party convention had tried to push as policy the kind of erotophobic ranting hitherto professed only by the wild-eyed goons on the margins of the new right, spouting chapter and verse from Revelations. Even if you thought the culture wars weren't over—they're not—and that *Sex* wasn't worth writing home about, it was still some kind of victory flag to fly over the broken arrows of the pitbull guardians of public moral-ity. As long as it lasts, let's rub their faces in perversion, and have it all bankrolled by the people who brought you Bugs Bunny (the barely closeted cartoon queer), no less.

There are good reasons for this euphoria. Madonna's book is the strange fruit of over twenty post-Stonewall years of sex radicalism, scarred and pitted by battles with left-wing as well as right-wing Puritanism, and nurtured by its uneasy bedfel-lowship with free market enterprise. The debates about plea-sure and danger with anti-porn feminists took a heavy toll, but by now the arguments on either side have more or less shaken down. While the anti-porn movement has made a much greater mark upon popular consciousness, it has won relatively few ad-herents among intellectuals in recent years. Less clear, as a problem of cultural politics, is the state of the union with a marketplace that professes no morality. For there is no doubt that the marketplace has played a crucial role in this most re-cent chapter of the history of left libertarianism.

What has come to be called identity politics (the semi-offi-cial forum for sexual politics) emerged and evolved in a capi-talist culture, partly as a dissenting response, but also partly as the product of a culture that circulates capital though the cre-ation of new market identities. Few, for example, would dispute that the disposable income of urban queers is of interest to con-sumer markets, or that it generates a good deal of consumer le-gitimacy as a result. To recognize the logic is not, of course, to salute it, for surely identity politics could have materialized in a different form in a different kind of society, cut from a differ-ent cloth. If wearing leather is all it takes, then Malcolm Forbes had a capitalist tool, too (he also wore a kilt, for what it's worth, to those of you who know what that means). At least one of the many cultural contradictions of capitalism is that anything, in theory, goes, even if it appears to challenge the stability of capital's conditions of reproduction. What Madonna has come to signify, for her legions of *advocates*, as distinct from her *fans*, is the principle that this contradiction can be genuinely exploited for sex-radical ends. Redeemer/Blasphemer, after all, is the favored double role of her semi-liturgical repertoire, on full display now in *Sex*: "I will raise you from the ground and without a sound you'll appear and surrender yourself to me, to love."

Because she has come to occupy such a large portion of public media attention, Madonna functions rather like what environmentalists call a charismatic megafauna: a highly visible, and lovable, species, like the whale or the spotted owl, in whose sympathetic name entire ecosystems can then be protected and safeguarded through public patronage. For sex radicals, Madonna now plays this role, as she herself has put it, of bringing "subversive sexuality into the mainstream," and has accepted the challenge for the most part, even reveling in the risk of her potential martyrdom as a celebrity. After all, if you live by the phallus, then you're likely to die by the phallus! Increasingly, the terms of her engagement have been more and more direct. Asked about homophobia in the music industry in a memorable 1991 *Advocate* interview, she retorted, "They're not going to be when I'm finished with them"; and, of Hollywood, "all these queens who are running this town should come out." In holy war terms, this was the militant speech of bitch/saint commitment, and the evidence of *Sex* is that Madonna has indeed found her cause—a public use for sex that she can call political, a bridge called her pussy. What can my pussy do for you? The invitation to "use me," in common with her customary range of S/M commands, has been interpreted quite liberally in the culture at large, where her narcissism has become a welcome vehicle for passengers en route to places along the way. Madonna, they all agree, is the best hope there is. (Of course, bedfellows sometimes make strange politics; in fact, they often do, if only because it can make for hot sex).

As a result, an awful lot of people have become invested in Madonna's fortunes in the business of making some kind of politics out of sex, or at least voyeurs of her progress in such a game with such high media stakes. Like royal-watchers, many have also become voyeurs of the apocalypse—How long can they/she last? If the British monarchy, force-fed with the oxygen of tabloid publicity, is increasingly the model for dysfunctional families (the pop princess, Diana, having taken the full toll of modernity upon her anthropologist husband—live by the scepter, die...), Madonna is regularly put to the test of demonstrating the principle of the survival of the sluttest. Unlike Marilyn, of whom we are partially persuaded that she did indeed live her life "like a candle in the wind," Madonna has been a superambient control queen when she is not living her life like a klieg light in a bathroom. With *Sex*, however, she has begun to close some doors, and not as a consequence of overexposure. Because of its commercially adult nature, *Sex* was the first Madonna production to restrict access to the prepubescent teen audience that once ran, hell for leather, into her fan factory. A friend's ten-year-old daughter, under the belly-buttoned spell of the Blond Ambitionist, asked me recently if there was anything in the book that a ten-year-old couldn't see. Now I have no earthly concept, myself, of what a ten-year-old should *not* see, although I do know that discussions about sexually controversial images are all too often hijacked by steering them onto the reef of children's sexuality, which parents have eternally suppressed. With her parents present, I thought it best to be coy in responding, while privately noting to myself that a child could probably make more sense of Madonna's "fantasies" than an adult could (at least, a child wouldn't suspect Madonna of not having the courage of her convictions, least of all suspect her of lacking even those convictions in the first place).

In a more prosaic afterthought, however, I realized that the book really was addressed to adults. Doesn't Smell Like Teen Spirit at all, in fact. Madonna's sophisticated offerings these days have very little to do with the willful clumsiness of grunge, the nervous speed of Riot Grrrls, the hyperkinetic trances of hardcore techno, the uncontoured vision quests of rave, or the baggy, jerky, dorky hieroglyphics of hip hop, let alone the electrically charged claustrophobia of prepubescent pop. Even in mall girl land, Madonna's most sustainable resource base of wannabes, the iron lawyers of youth taste are striking a different pose, just at the moment that lipstick feminism is getting around to approving the politics of cosmetic tartiness for all young lipsinkas of the Puberty Blues. In the age of the supermodel, where Claudia, Cindy, Naomi, Christy, Nicky, Linda, Elle and the rest of the aristocracy are more familiar daily presences than our best friends—Look Like a Model, Don't Think Like One—the emergent style is embodied in the gangly, Plain Jane look of Kristen McMenamy, or Kate Moss, a crucial presence in the style bible, *The Face*, until she was propelled into the global realm of billboard visibility by Calvin Klein. Her booking agent puts it this way: "She is entirely without artifice. She looks like there's hope." A marketed symptom, then, of the decadennial do-si-do between artifice and nature, the cockney Moss is, among other things, a reissued Twiggy of the nineties, eschewing the eighties heady romp around the catwalk of inauthenticity. She is supposed to signal the end of the grand mistress narratives. She doesn't work it, she doesn't even work, really. By contrast, Madonna may already be too sexy for this decade.

While she shares the logic of the supermodel in integrating the various culture industries—advertising, film, music, fashion, TV, publishing—Madonna is also heir to the decade when the producer and the D.J. took corporate command, respectively, of the recording studio and the dance floor. Consequently, she runs her own Good Ship LolliPop, including a spanking new record label, but the passengers are becoming more and more exclusive. Indeed, Madonna's most regular port of call has been Downtown clubland, and for most of the time *Sex* is pretty much moored up there. The Gaiety Boys burlesque, the sleaze chambers of the Vault, the unclassified ads for sex tramp posturing, the terminally hip fashion victims, the safety-in-numbers dragsy repertoire of bleach blond Metropolitania. The images of this scene are actually a suburbanite's idea of the decadent underground city life, internalized and repackaged as an urban swinger's idea of home, sweet home. Phallus in Wonderland. A way-off-Broadway staging of nuclear familialism, featuring the perversions wrought by daddy fetishism, sibling cannibalism, child molesting, cousin kissing, phallic mothering, and all too free brotherly love. Even if the Madonnacentrism of *Sex* leaves out the warm communitarian feel of the dance floor, this is still great propaganda for the bad good life, for Alternative America, and all that. So rife is the *metropolitanism*, however, that it complements this view of the city by returning its images of the nonmetropole to the suburbanite in an alienated form. Nowhere is this more evident than in the presentation of what is supposed to be the hip New Yorker's view of life beyond the bridge and tunnel, where white-trashism, especially, is given a questionable camp reception.

Most memorable, and most downright draggish, is Madonna's version of a suburban Miami floozy, with an unruly blond wig, Maud Frizon heels, and handbag, padding around in the buff on the lawn, and cradling, not the dipso's Wild Turkey, but the material girl's trademark Evian. Here is the Madonna who, in her suburban New York incarnation, guested famously and discreetly on *Saturday Night Live*'s "Coffee Talk" in one of the all-time-great middle-brow testaments to Streisandesque divadom. This is also the sequence that contains the probably immortal hitchhiker shot, an updating and upstaging of Marilyn and her billowing dress on the subway grating. Hitchhiking will not be quite the same after this. It was once the emblematic activity of youth straining at the parental leash to be out on the road and looking for America. Then it became a standard plot device of the thriller or horror road movie. Then it became condensed, as an iconic activity for post-punk times, into the hooker routine of thumbing a ride around the block. But in this image, Madonna is not lighting out for the open road—she is heading into town. Equally, there's no psychokiller undercurrent—everything is as it seems. Nor is she out on the streetwalker's day shift—this is a bright suburban highway, not a dim dockside alleyway. Besides, her attitude, and there's plenty of it, points elsewhere. But where? She's going shopping. What for? For clothes. Why? It's late afternoon (you can tell by the shadows), and the stores will be closing soon. How? By bus, although she's not anywhere near a bus stop. And who is she anyway? A would-have-been Jewish American Princess, a fading Hollywood hopeful, or an upscale bag-lady who thinks that paying her taxes entitles her to full naked use of her city's public domain.

This is also Madonna's favorite photo: "It was very liberating," she says. "I felt really free. It's the most unpermissible thing. You're not supposed to be out in public without your clothes on, and yet there wasn't anything sexual about it. I couldn't stop giggling, the looks on these people's faces when they would drive by. I just had the best time." Told that in the picture she resembles Dietrich, she replies, "Dietrich? She *wishes*." The least bitchy interpretation of this comment is to assume that the reference is not to the superiority of Madonna's body—a study in white girl iconography for which she has literally worked her butt off—but rather that the reference is to the "unpermissibility"—something to which Dietrich herself might have aspired had the moral climate in her day been more propitious. The comparison sets free other thoughts, however, about the history of gay iconography. The key to Dietrich's smoky presence was not that she had a particular knack for cross-dressing (she didn't really), but rather that she hit upon a formulaic pose—in *The Blue Angel*—that could be impersonated unmistakably. This is one of the secrets of camp imagery; when it works well, it is so locked into the culture's memory codes that it has to be copied (and caricatured) almost immediately, or else it is lost to history. Within a week, the first, and most completely understood, cover version of the Madonna hitchhiker appeared in Michael Musto's *Village Voice* parody. Ann Magnuson's parody of *Sex*, called *Wank*, involving a housewife in a zipper mask carrying white bread on a tray, appeared not long after in *Paper* magazine. A memorable mural by Howie Zeck graced the cruising lounge of the Sound Factory, downtown's temple of dance worship. The rest is more than just history; it's the ceaseless process of recovery and renovation.

In speculating about other, more historical examples of this mechanism of recovery, I was reminded of the often-cited observation that Madonna is the best known woman in the world. The Statue of Liberty, the example I came up with, is probably the most well-known female figure in the world. Almost from the beginning, the statue was being retrieved from the State, because people could see that it was something that they should not be required to look up to. Lady Liberty much too literally stood for something, which made it impossible to resist adopting her as a stand-in for anyone and everything, from ads for cooking oil to posters against Yankee imperialism. On the one hand, she was seen to be wearing the emperor's new clothes (doric ones); on the other hand, she was of foreign origin, a potential safeguard for what Pierre Clastres called "society against the state." Liberty, then, was the original Politically Correct girl, though hardly the Lady of Permissions, at least not in the way that we understand modern libertarianism. Which is what makes Madonna's comments—"it's the most unpermissible thing"—about the disrobed figure (it doesn't have to be female) particularly evocative if you consider the figure against the backdrop of Lady Liberty: "there wasn't anything sexual about it."

If there's any truth to that statement, as applied to that image, then the Hitchhiker does not automatically belong in the sequence of public feminist iconography that originates with the crowning of a live sheep at the 1968 protests against the Miss America Pageant. More recently, that sequence has included Madonna's own crotch grab for a 1989 cover of *Interview*, Demi Moore's pregnancy portrait for *Vanity Fair*, Linda Hamilton's hardbody in *Terminator 2*, Grace Jones's cyborg body still everywhere, and Annie Lennox's and k.d. lang's panoply of cross-dressings. The power of such images, pushed into the foreground of commercial visibility, is easily analyzed by the sort of liberal media commentary that registers and acknowledges how far women are going these days. Madonna's photograph does not sit so easily with that school of image analysis.

Such an analysis, for example, might ask the following questions of the Hitchhiker shot. Is this a libertarian image that seizes permission for the female body? Insofar as it represents public space being reclaimed boldly by a woman who believes that indiscretion is the better part of valor, I would say yes. And is there anything sexual about it? By which Madonna probably means, does it exploit her body sexually? Insofar as its humor depends upon her nudity but not upon her gender, the answer is surely no. Is it a strong statement, then, about female sexuality? Yes, again, if that means making a woman a fully active agent in the presentation of her bodily appearance. And is it gay-positive? Most certainly, whether or not you are reminded of Dietrich.

But these questions and answers belong to the language and mental landscape of political correctness. They will only get you so far along this road, although for Madonna, such questions and the people who ask them have become fellow travelers in recent years, if not bedfellows (at least as far as we know). But the whole point of *Sex* is that it deliberately strays from the definition of erotica that politically correct anti-porn feminism used to espouse as a fine-art antidote to hardcore pornography—healthy, wholesome Carole King sex: no power plays, no sleaze, no bad girl stuff. To be sure, there are images in Madonna's book that evoke fine-art settings, whether religious, like the altarpiece Passion play in which she is suspended over the ocean, or pagan, like the monumental fountain shot (although it otherwise evokes female ejaculation, the great open secret of lesbian subculture in the early nineties). But for the most part the book is supposed to be on the side of bad art and good politics, and those who favor this winning combination know that Madonna is down with them. If you leave aside Cindy Sherman, the Hitchhiker harbors no fine-art allusions (although, by citing Lady Liberty, I suppose I have conjured up, in my own mind at least, Delacroix's famous *Liberté* that Bartholdi was under pressure not to emulate—it was thought to be too subversive. And there is a history of libertinism that links the Delacroix with the Hitchhiker). For the most part, it's fair to say, however, that the Hitchhiker drops straight out of the relentless climate of North American popular culture. If it's not really about the life of the road—a staple narrative of demotic culture—it's still a warped anthem to mobility, upward or downward, depending on how you see it.

As it happens, the hardass "I've got mine" attitude and the tenacious, white-knuckled grip on that handbag are defiantly at odds with a genteel culture of property. It's the same attitude that produces bag ladies of all classes, from the streetwise homeless to the Leona Helmsleys of Park Ave; indeed, Madonna's own nervy status as a populist mogul prepared to defend her every move and every real estate purchase owes a lot to the same highly public neurosis about the ultimate value of personal property in this society. The sense of liability attached to the public life of property operates well above or well below the terminal emotional velocity achieved by the grand narratives of bourgeois stability in other societies which try to render discreet their aristocratic histories. Here, by contrast, the guilt can be stripped clean, but people still want to show it off. Or else, they go overboard on compensation, brazenly insisting on self-entitlement even when all they have are the shoes on their feet. These dual responses function like default settings in American popular culture, even in daily life; you don't have to look very hard among your friends, or your enemies, to watch them kick in.

So Madonna is only half right about the nudity in this picture; there's isn't anything sexual about it, true, but there's nothing so simple here as a woman's bold seizure of the codes of exhibitionism or permissibility. And, excuse me, she may be smoking the brand, but this is not a Virginia Slims cigarette ad. What we have instead is a nude study in the psychopathology of economics; the problem, quite literally, of how to dress for success. Primarily, but not exclusively, a women's issue in our times, here treated to the same savage burlesque that many watchers have seen behind Madonna's celebrated progression from Boytoy to Material Girl to Vamporama. Feminists have rightfully been ambivalent about this game of dress-up/down, wondering whether this is indeed the work of an artful dodger, or whether it's just another ad for late capitalism that says "you've come a long way, baby." By now, of course, this debate is wearing a little thin. As much as anything, it was a debate about the soul of postmodernism, or more precisely, about whether postmodernism had any soul at all. For every old school nonbeliever turned off by the artifice and the worship of surfaces, there was a Madonna evangelist devoutly arguing the case for the supreme pontifical power of inauthenticity. To cut a long story short, the Madonna debate turned into a medium for arguing that postmodern feminism didn't have to be post-feminist. Put this way, it doesn't sound like much to argue, but, for many younger feminists, winning the Madonna wars was tantamount to declaring a politics which did not deny itself a life of pleasure and style and bleached eyebrows. Feminism, they said, shouldn't be utilitarian in its recruitism; it ought to be conversant with the fantasy-struck language of daily life. Madonna, of course, happened to be in the right place at the right time.

(One last, important thing about the Hitchhiker image. There's more than a hint of craziness here, the famous American craziness that non-Americans like me are supposed to take great delight in seeing everywhere, but which can hardly be considered a national secret when you see so many naked peo-ple out on the streets—a not uncommon sight in this desperate culture. Behavior like this is considered to be a normative part of the North American urban landscape, considered to be a genuine expression, in some way, of American liberties. Al-though this is not the time and place to do it, the analysis of American "craziness," like British "eccentricity," deserves ex-tensive study as part of some broad behavioral history of the national culture in its specific class and racial formation. It would be a study that could explain these respective codes of conduct as responses to the forced assimilation of so many di-asporic margins in the one case-history, in contrast with the rigorously exported world-view of the metropolitan center in the other. Nakedness has its place in both histories; the need to be naked in public is a highly social perversion, drenched with the hemorrhage of consensus. Madonna's shot at making erot-ica, even at its most socially unconscious, as in this image, nonetheless feeds into the political history of American psy-chopathology.)

It would be foolish, however, to discount Madonna's own exhibitionism and her intensive choreographing of media responses to her public narcissism, because they are a crucial element of the power she enjoys in her role as what sociologists call a style leader or tastemaker. The V-8 engine of her own narcissism has put her so far out in front of the pack that a profile of her as a "crazy woman" has begun to displace that of the control queen in limited sectors of popular consciousness. It can't be long, a certain logic goes, before she enters Elvisland, and people begin to see her face in a crater on the moon. However unlikely this scenario, it would be the end of a very strange chapter in cultural politics, when a female pop singer came to be the vehicle for the political hopes of so many marginalized communities. The story told in that chapter is a little different from the codes of entertainment politics activated whenever "liberal Hollywood" turns out for a campaign stop or an inaugural ball, or when rock performers play a benefit for this or that cause. Back in the embryonic days of glitter rock, David Bowie's public admissions of bisexuality (circa 1972) helped to clear the air and ease the way for many gay people, but no one expected him to play any role whatsoever in the movement for gay and lesbian rights. By contrast, the demands made of Madonna have been based on broader expectations because they come from an advanced understanding of what it is that entertainers can and cannot do in the business of what might be called *cultural justice* ("culturally just": a suggested alternative term for "politically correct"?). This latitude has something to do with Madonna's transcendence of the rock/pop split (rock artists are conventionally obliged to have views about politics, pop artists are not) but it ultimately derives from activities other than making ads for Rock the Vote—"freedom of speech is as good as sex"—or doing the right thing for AIDS funding. Indeed, this kind of cultural power is seldom so articulate because it is based upon confidential agreements that audiences pretend to enjoy with performers, and that performers do their best to acknowledge in a suitably clandestine way. Madonna is now partly in the business of openly recognizing these contracts. This is why, when they see her, certain sectors of her audience can only see a savvy entrepreneur flaunting her body like the tart she otherwise must surely not want to be, while other sectors see her performances, bizarre as it may still sound, as a continuation of identity politics by other means.

This strikes me as a rather important moment in the history of popular culture, and well worth the discussion. In particular, one of the concerns of this essay is to understand why the affinity-style loyalties that are currently associated with the name of Madonna only extend into certain communities, and are considered a liability in others. Unlike most white performers, Madonna has never had to rely upon siphoning off credibility from the central reservoirs of African American music and culture. There's little evidence that she, unlike most white performers, has ever thought that she was black. The throaty slow rapping she slurs through on parts of the *Erotica* album sounds more like a cross between a druggy phone sex monologue and a film noir voiceover than any conventional rip-off of rap rhymes. Rather, she has drawn sporadically from the margins of gay black experience and from whitegirl fantasies about the ethical grace of Latino masculinity. Much criticized as exercises in subcultural tourism, these are cultural bridges nonetheless; avenues where white female sexuality can hitch a ride in relative safety. Who knows, finally, what straight men (of whatever color) who see her as a sexual object think about her version of Pussy Power—an autocracy that demands attention to sexual diversity. No doubt it captures their attention, and perhaps it questions their disrespect, and there's even a chance that it forms a queer bridge over the panicky intersection that passes for heterosexuality these days.

But when it comes to the tribal identification demanded by *their* peers, Madonna's musical persona enjoys little loyalty. Thrash, power metal and hardcore rap govern the field. The black dick, in particular, commands allegiance from audiences that the white pussy cannot. In Tijuana, in January 1993, I saw Ice-T sing with Body Count. It was not a particularly memorable concert (Ice-T was hoarse, and he didn't seem to realize that he was in Mexico), except for Ice-T's virtuoso presentation of "Evil Dick" in which he paid a semi-parodic tribute to the adolescent male religion of jacking off, by careening around the stage and fucking the floor while furiously stroking an imaginary outsized penis. This awkward frenzy of masturbation is the staple erotic rhythm of whiteboy thrash and hardcore music, and Ice-T's theatrical take on the ritual was a calculated component of the crossover experiment of Body Count. But, in the ultimate fuck you, he also reminded his audience of the semi-official cultural status of the black penis as public enemy number one, one of the longest running fantasies of the North American nation state. Nothing so plucky could have been attempted on the hardcore hip hop stage. It was only by vaulting over the barriers of musical apartheid that the rapper could perform this burlesque of masculinity that brought the house down. In her own not unrelated way, Madonna has taken the gambit of sexuality onto a different stage, hurdling a different set of barriers.

What Ice-T does with his evil dick in thrash, what Madonna does with her pussy with nine lives in erotica, these are the public spectacles of our times, charged with the legacy of what Elvis did with his hips in 1956. The formations of race, sexuality, and gender that were fused together in the torso movements of a Southern whiteboy almost forty years ago have spun apart, separately and, as always, unequally, in the intervening decades. It is not necessary, but it may be useful to see Madonna's ascendancy alongside the rise to prominence of hardcore rapper masculinity. In many ways, they are part of the same cultural moment, even though the dialogue between them is probably not the first thing most folks would stop to consider.

There is nothing arbitrary about the line of demarcation that separates Madonna's domain from that of Ice-T. It is as historically powerful as anything in our culture right now. No doubt it can be aligned with larger patterns of institutional racism, sexism and homophobia in society and the music industry, but it cannot be easily transcended by a direct attack on these structural prejudices. Musical culture, in particular, has all sorts of genres and conventions for mediating the prejudices; it even has conventions for converting prejudices into convictions of taste, precisely those convictions through which fan loyalty is won and maintained. The most skilled interpreters of the rules, like Madonna herself, will always disappoint us since we always expect too much of them. Asking Madonna to justify your love may be more useful, in the long run, than scolding her for "not doing enough." For one thing, you'll get more attention. And according to the rules of fanthink, you may even get lucky.

bell hooks

# Power to the Pussy: We Don't Wannabe Dicks in Drag

*"I believe in the power of Madonna, that she has the
balls to be the patron saint of new feminism."*
—Kate Tentler, The Village Voice

In my twenties, I made my first pilgrimage to Europe. Journey-
ing there was a necessary initiation for any young artist in the
United States destined to lead a Bohemian life of intensity, a life
on the edge, full of adventure. Nothing about being black, female, working class, growing up in a racially segregated southern town, where the closest I ever came to ecstasy was during
Sunday morning church service, made me think that the doors
of avant garde radical cool would be closed to me. Confined and
restrained by family, region, and religion, I was inwardly homeless, suffering, I believed, from a heartbreaking estrangement
from a divine community of radical artistic visionaries whom I
imagined were longing for me to join them. In much pain,
I spent my childhood years dreaming of the moment when I
would find my way home. In my imagination, home was a place
of radical openness, of recognition and reconciliation, where
one could create freely.

Europe was a necessary starting place for this search. I believed I would not find there the dehumanizing racism so pervasive here that it crippled black creativity. The Europe of my
imagination was a place of artistic and cultural freedom, where
there were no limits or boundaries. I had learned about this Europe in books, in the writings of black expatriates. Yet this was
not the Europe I discovered. The Europe I journeyed to was a
place where racism was ever present, only it took the form of a
passion for the "primitive," the "exotic." When a friend and I

**65**

arrived in Paris, a taxi driver took us to a hotel where pictures of nude black females adorned the walls. Everywhere, I encountered the acceptance and celebration of blackness as long as it remained within the confines of primitivism.

Ironically, white Europeans were constantly urging me to join them in their affirmation of Europe as a more free, less racist, more culturally open place than the United States. At some point I was told that Europeans, unlike white Americans, had no trouble worshipping a black Madonna; this was proof that their culture was able to move beyond race and racism. Indeed, European friends insisted that I make a pilgrimage to Montserrat to see for myself. At the shrine of the black Madonna I saw long lines of adoring white worshippers offering homage. They were praying, crying, longing to caress and touch, to be blessed by this mysterious black woman saint. In their imaginations her presence was the perfect embodiment of the miraculous. To be with her was to be in the place of ecstasy. Indeed, momentarily in this sanctuary, race, class, gender and nationality had fallen away. In their place was a vision of hope and possibility. Yet this moment in no way altered the politics of domination outside, in that space of the real. Only in the realm of the sacred imaginary was there the possibility of transcendence. None of us could remain there.

My journey ended. I did not return home to become a Bohemian artist. My creative work, painting and writing, was pushed to the background as I worked hard to succeed in the academy, to become something I had never wanted to be. To this day I feel as imprisoned in the academic world as I felt in the world of my growing up. And I still cling to the dream of a radical visionary artistic community that can sustain and nurture creativity.

I share these memories and reflections as a preface to talking about Madonna as a cultural icon, to contextualize what she has represented for me. Early on, I was enamored of her not so much because I was "into" her music—I was into her presence. Her image, like that of the black Madonna, evoked a sense of promise and possibility, a vision of freedom; feminist in that she was daring to transgress sexist boundaries; Bohemian in that she was an adventurer, a risk taker; daring in that she presented a complex non-static ever changing subjectivity. She was intense, into pleasure yet disciplined. For me and many other young "hip" feminist women confined in the academy, Madonna was a symbol of unrepressed female creativity and power—sexy, seductive, serious, and strong. She was the embodiment of that radical risk-taking part of my/our female self that had to be repressed daily for us to make it in the institutionalized world of the mainstream, in the academy. For a long while, her transgressive presence was a beacon, a guiding light, charting the journey of female "feminist" artists coming to power—coming to cultural fulfillment.

These days, watching Madonna publicly redefine her persona away from this early politicized image of transgressive female artistry necessarily engenders in diverse feminist admirers feelings of betrayal and loss. We longed to witness the material girl enter mature womanhood still embodying a subversive feminist spirit. We longed for this, in part, to see serious radical female cultural icons manifesting the feminist promise that sexism would not always limit, inform, and shape our cultural identities and destiny. Deep down, many feminist Madonna admirers, ourselves entering mature womanhood, fear that this transition will signal the end of all forms of radicalism—social, sexual, cultural. We have so needed her transgressions. Women struggling to maintain fierce commitment to radical feminist womanhood in the face of a culture that rewards betrayal want to have a feminist icon who stands against the patriarchy, who "fights the power." For a long time, Madonna appeared to be that icon. Since feminist thinking and the feminist movement are currently undermined by intense backlash, we long for female icons who show everyone that we can triumph despite fierce anti-feminism. Ultimately, we know that feminist transformation of culture and society is even more directly threatened when those who were once advocates, supporters of feminist demands for an end to sexism and sexist oppression, act as though this is no longer a necessary and crucial agenda. Hence, our collective lament when it appears that Madonna will not fulfill that earlier sense of feminist promise and power.

Currently, Madonna is redefining her public persona in a manner that negates and erases her earlier support for feminist issues. The first hint of this major about-face was made public in the October 1992 issue of *Vanity Fair* with its display of Madonna as little girl sex kitten. A frightening gap separated the radical vision of active female sexuality Madonna projects in the *Vanity Fair* interview with Maureen Orth (evocatively titled "The Material Girl's Sexual (R)Evolution") and the boring, conventional kiddie-porn type photographs accompanying the text. The image of a grown, over thirty, Madonna recreating herself as a little girl sex kitten, presumably for the thrill of gaining and holding onto the sustained mass patriarchal pornographic gaze for as long as she can keep the public's attention, exposes the way female aging in a sexist society can undermine any woman's allegiance to radical politics, to feminism. What is "the material girl" to do when she has fast become a grown woman in an economy of cultural images where so much of her mass appeal was deeply rooted in the romance of rebellious youth? The re-creation of herself as little girl comes across primarily as an opportunistic attempt to sustain the image that she can be forever young. Starting over again as little-girl-on-the-playground sex symbol, Madonna abandons and betrays her earlier radical questioning of sexist objectifications of female sexuality, announcing via these photos that she consents to being represented within a field of image production that is overdetermined by patriarchy and the needs of a heterosexist pornographic gaze.

Gone is the "hot" Madonna who dares to challenge the status quo. There is nothing "fierce" or even interesting about the *Vanity Fair* photographs. And they do not evoke in me fierce response. Looking at them I just simply felt sad. After all her daring, her courageous challenging of sexist constructions of female sexuality, Madonna at the peak of her power has stopped pushing against the system. Her new image has no radical edge. The loss of that subversive style is all the more evident in *Sex*. Suddenly, nothing about Madonna's image is politicized. Instead, with the publication of *Sex*, she assumes the role of high priestess of a cultural hedonism that seeks to substitute unlimited production and pursuit of sexual pleasure for a radical, liberating political practice, one that would free our minds and our bodies.

*Sex* pushes pervasive hedonism as an alternative to resistance. The shifting radical subjectivity that was the quintessential trademark of Madonna's earlier opposition to conformist fixed identity was a daring to be different that was not expressive of shallow exhibitionism but of a will to confront, challenge, and change the status quo. I remember Madonna flaunting sexual assertiveness in early videos like "Material Girl," telling *Nightline* that she drew the line at violence, humiliation and degradation of women. It is this subject position that has disappeared. As Susan Bordo reminds us in her essay "Material Girl: The Effacements of Postmodern Culture," that will to be different "is won through ongoing political struggle rather than through the act of creative interpretation." Ironically, it is precisely at this cultural moment when Madonna allies herself with the status quo that she insists on identifying herself as radical, declaring, "I see myself as a revolutionary at this point." She asserts her belief that *Sex* will function politically, that it will "open some people's minds," presumably that it will lead viewers to accept and condone various sexual practices. The irony is, of course, that for those viewers who have always consumed a range of patriarchal pornographic material and/or progressive erotica, *Sex* offers no new images. Every time I open *Sex* I am reminded of a high school yearbook. The layout and design appear amateurish. Constant changing of type face and style, etc. evoke memories of meetings about my high school yearbook where we just agreed that anything goes and let everyone's desires be represented. This casual effect seems highly intentional in *Sex*. Where the faces of graduating seniors and their classmates might be, Madonna gives us diverse sexual images, many of which look as though they have been appropriated from *Players, Playboy, On Our Backs* and so on, with of course one special difference—they all feature Madonna.

While this in-your-face collection of porn and erotica may seduce a mass public (particularly an audience of teenaged consumers) that might never have gone seeking these images in the many other places where they could be found, it is doubtful that it will change anyone's view about sexual practice. Despite Madonna's hype that would have the public believe she is the radical visionary introducing transgressive subject matter to a mass audience, the reality is that advertisements, videos, movies, and television were already exploiting these images. Madonna is really only a link in the marketing chain that exploits representations of sexuality and the body for profit, a chain which focuses on images that were once deemed "taboo." Not wanting to undermine her own hype, the material girl must argue that her images are different—original. The major difference, of course, is that the space she occupies as cultural entertainer and icon enables her to reach a much larger audience than traditional consumers of pornographic images or progressive erotica. Despite her hopes of radical intervention, the vast majority of readers seem to approach *Sex* like conventional consumers of pornography. The book is used to sexually excite, provoke, or stimulate voyeuristic masturbatory pleasure. Nothing radical about that.

The most radical aspect of *Sex* is its appropriation and use of homoerotic imagery. This use is not unique. Commenting on the way these acts of appropriation have become a new trend, *Newsweek*'s review of *Sex* asserted: "As gay-bashing has become one of the most common hate-crimes in America, gay iconography is bubbling up defiantly in mainstream media. Since Madonna first cast herself as Marilyn Monroe, she has played out the role of drag queen, using identity as a form of self-defense. In exchange for her genuine affection, she's raided gay subculture's closet for the best of her ideas. Like Klein, she isn't just taking explicit sex mainstream; she is taking explicit homosex mainstream. In this she is a pioneer. Hard as it is to imagine a major celebrity of another era making a book as graphic as *Sex*, and surviving—it's impossible to imagine anyone making one as gay." In other words, within today's cannibalistic market economy the willingness to consume homoerotic and/or homosexual images does not correspond to a cultural willingness to stand against homophobia or challenge heterosexism.

Patriarchal pornography has always appropriated and exploited homoeroticism. Within the larger context of pornographic sexual hedonism anything goes—and all taboos become part of the pleasure mix. This experience does not mean that the individuals consuming these images are not fiercely committed to maintaining heterosexism and perpetuating homophobia. Voyeuristic desire to look at, or experience through fantasy, sexual practices that in one's everyday life might be perceived as taboo does not signal a rupture in the sexual status quo. That is why simply portraying these images, mass marketing them to a larger public is in and of itself not a subversive intervention, though in some instances it may have a disruptive challenging impact.

Throughout Madonna's career she has appropriated fascinating aspects of gay subcultures even as she has often framed gay experience in a stereotypically heterosexist and homophobic manner. (An example of this tendency is her insistence in the film *Truth or Dare* that her dancers, most of whom are gay and non-white, are "emotional cripples" who need her to "play mother," guiding and disciplining them.) This kind of maternal/paternalism fits with a history of so-called sympathetic heterosexual framing of homosexual experience in popular culture which represents it as deviant, subversive, wild, a "horror" that is both fascinating and fun but always fundamentally a "horror."

This unsubversive manner of representation jumps out from the pages of *Sex*. The initial pictures of Madonna with two lesbian sex radicals portrays them in scenarios that visually construct them as freaks. In various shots Madonna is positioned in relation to them in a manner that insists on the primacy of her image as the embodiment of a heterosexual norm, "the ideal feminine." Visually placed in several photographs as voyeur and/or victim, she is at the center and the lesbian couple always marginalized. Homophobic constructions of gay sexual practice in mass media consistently reinforce the stereotypical notion that gay folks are predators, eager to feast upon the innocent. Madonna is the symbol of innocence; the two lesbian women represent experience. Unlike her, they do not have firm hard bodies, or wear on their faces the freshly made-up, well-fed all-American look. One of the most powerful non-erotic or pornographic images in this sequence shows Madonna at a distance from the two women, looking anguished as though she does not belong, as though being in their presence hurts. A study in contrast, Madonna consistently appears in these images as though she is with them but not of them. Posed in this way, her presence invites status quo readers to imagine that they too can consume images of difference, participate in the sexual practices depicted, and yet remain untouched—unchanged.

Embodying the highest expression of capitalist patriarchal pornographic power, Madonna emerges in *Sex* as the penultimate sexual voyeur. She looks, then asks that we look at her looking. Since all the while the literate reader of her opening remarks knows that we are not really seeing documentary photos but a carefully constructed sexual stage, we can never forget that our gaze is directed, controlled. We have paid for our right to look, just as Madonna has paid the two women to appear with her. Our gaze must always and only be directed at what she wants us to see. And this means that what appears to be a portrait of homoeroticism/homosexuality is merely a reflection of her voyeuristic perspective. It is that overdetermining perspective that shapes and informs the image of gay sexual practice we are allowed to see.

Within the sphere of Madonna's pornographic gaze, gayness is re-inscribed as a trope within the cultural narrative of patriarchal pornographic sexual hedonism. The gayness presented throughout *Sex* does not call for a recognition and acceptance of difference. It is instead a demand that difference be appropriated in a manner that diffuses its power. Hence, the consuming voyeuristic pornographic gaze violates the gay body and being by suggesting, via the mode of appropriation, that the site of interrogation must always rest not with the homoerotic/homosexual presence but with a heterosexual center. Gayness then appears as merely an extension of heterosexual pleasure, part of that practice and not an alternative or fundamentally different expression of sexual desire.

Ultimately, images of homosexuality in *Sex*, though presented as never before to a mainstream audience, are not depicted in a manner that requires viewers to show any allegiance to, or understanding of, the context from which they emerge. Indeed, they are presented as though they come into being through the heterosexual imagination, thereby enabling heterosexual and/or homophobic audiences to share in Madonna's voyeuristic relations, looking into and at "gayness," without connecting that pleasure to any resistance struggle for gay rights, to any demand that they relinquish heterosexist power. As with the opening pages, the image of Madonna in a gay club surrounded by men evokes a will to violate—to enter a space that is at the very least symbolically, if not actually closed—off limits. Even in the realm of male homoeroticism/homosexuality Madonna's image usurps, takes over, subordinates. Coded always in *Sex* as heterosexual, her image is the dominant expression of heterosexism. Mirroring the role of a plantation overseer in a slave-based economy, Madonna surveys the landscape of sexual hedonism, her "gay" freedom, her territory of the other, her jungle. No break with stereotypes here. And more importantly, no critical interrogation of the way in which these images perpetuate and maintain institutionalized homophobic domination. In the context of *Sex*, gay culture remains irrevocably linked to a system of patriarchal control framed by a heterosexist pornographic gaze.

Just as representations of gayness are not problematized in *Sex*, neither is S/M. No longer an underground happening, S/M scenarios are among the sexual taboos exploited for profit. Such scenarios are now commonly enacted on prime time television shows and in movies. Yet none of what we see in mainstream media (*Sex* is no exception) shows images of sex radicals who are committed to a vision of sexual pleasure that rests on mutual consent. Consent comes through communication. Yet the S/M we see both in mainstream media and in *Sex* is not about consent. It is the subject-to-subject dimension of S/M that is lost when symbols of these sexual practices are appropriated to shock or titillate. None of Madonna's fictive S/M monologues foreground issues of agreement and consent. In both images and written text, S/M is represented solely as being about punishment. Narrow notions of sexual sadomasochism fail to characterize it as a sexual ritual that "works" issues of pain and power. Whatever the degree of punishment present, the point is ultimately pleasure.

In her all-knowing rap on S/M, Madonna assumes the role of teacher/authority, giving us truth learned from an authentic source: "I talked to a dominatrix once and she said the definition of S/M was that you let someone hurt you who you know would never hurt you. It's always a mutual choice. You have an unstated agreement between you." Yet in Madonna's mind the choice is always to hurt or be hurt. It is this perversion of sex-radical practice that informs her assertion: "I don't even think S/M is about sex. I think it's about power, the struggle for power." While S/M is about power, it's about negotiation—the antithesis of competitive struggle.

By placing herself in the role of instructor and selling *Sex* as a how-to manual, Madonna dangerously usurps the progressive voices and bodies of diverse individuals engaged in S/M sexual practice. Her most reactionary take on S/M conflates heterosexual male violence against women with consensual sadomasochism. Prefacing her brief discussion of S/M, Madonna asserts: "I think for the most part if women are in an abusive relationship and they know it and they stay in it, they must be digging it. I suppose some people might think that's an irresponsible statement. I'm sure there are a lot of women in abusive relationships who don't want to be, who are trapped economically; they have all these kids and they have to deal with it. But I have friends who have money and are educated and they stay in abusive relationships, so they must be getting something out of it." Revealing that she is no expert on domestic violence, Madonna flaunts her ignorance with the same seductive arrogance of sexist men who have used the same faulty logic to condone, support, and perpetuate violence against women.

More than any visual image in *Sex* these remarks signal Madonna's break with feminist thinking. Reflecting a patriarchal standpoint, these statements are more than just irresponsible; they are dangerous. Madonna uses her position as cultural icon to sanction violence against women. And the tragedy of it all is that these statements are inserted in an utterly gratuitous manner. They are in no way connected to the visual images of heterosexual S/M. By making them, Madonna uses *Sex* as a platform to express right-wing anti-feminist sentiments that, if uttered in another context, might have provoked public protest and outrage.

Concluding her declaration with the insistence that "the difference between abuse and S/M is the issue of responsibility," Madonna neatly deflects attention away from the real issue of "choice." To focus on choice rather than responsibility she would have had to acknowledge that within patriarchal culture where male domination of women is promoted and male physical and sexual abuse of women is socially sanctioned, no open cultural climate exists to promote consensual heterosexual power play, in any arena, and that includes the sexual. Few women have the freedom to choose an S/M sexual practice in a heterosexual relationship. Contrary to Madonna's assertions, female class power rarely mediates male violence, even though it may offer a means of escape. No doubt Madonna knows this, but she is more concerned with courting and seducing an anti-feminist public, a misogynist sexist audience that makes exactly the same pronouncements about women and abuse. A similar critique could be made of Madonna's comments on pornography.

Madonna's appropriation of gayness as the sign of transgression, as well as her preoccupation with S/M, usually deflects attention away from her use of racially charged imagery. Critics who applaud the way she draws mainstream attention to gay sexuality say nothing about the issue of race. Yet the cultural narrative of white supremacy is woven throughout the visual and written text of *Sex*. Despite her personal history as dark ethnic from an immigrant background, Madonna's megasuccess is tied to her representation as a blonde. By assuming the mantle of Marilyn Monroe, she publicly revealed her longing to leave behind the experience of her ethnic and bodily history to inhabit the cultural space of the white feminine ideal. In his essay "White," film critic Richard Dyer describes the way

Hollywood's idealization of white femininity converges with aesthetic standards informed by white supremacy. Emphasizing that the image of Monroe "is an inescapably and necessarily white one," Dyer calls attention to the fact that "the codes of glamour lighting in Hollywood were developed in relation to white women, to endow them with a glow and radiance that has correspondence with the transcendental rhetoric of popular Christianity." Significantly, only "white"-skinned females could be imagined as innocent, virtuous, transcendent. This fact affirms my white European friends' assertion that there is no cultural space within the United States that would allow white folks to deify black femaleness, to worship a black Madonna. Racism and sexism combine to make it impossible for white folks, and even some black folks, to imagine a black Madonna, since such figures are representations of purity and innocence. Within racist and sexist iconography the black female is stereotypically portrayed as experienced and impure. Hence, she can never embody that Birth of a Nation fragile womanhood that is the essence of a Madonna figure.

Within white supremacist culture, a female must be white to occupy the space of sacred femininity, and she must also be blond. Prior to the shooting of images in *Sex*, Madonna had returned to her natural dark hair color. Yet workers helping to construct her public persona insisted that she bleach her hair blond. *Entertainment Weekly* reported that Madonna was reluctant, but that she was told by her make-up artist: "This is your book. If you want to want to be a brunette, fine. But in black and white, blond magnifies better. Blond *says more!*" Blond speaks, says more, when it both mirrors and embodies the white supremacist aesthetics that inform the popular imagination of our culture. Concurrently, Madonna's appropriation of the identity of the European actress Dita and of her Germanic couture is an obvious gesture connecting her to a culture of fascism, Nazism, and white supremacy, particularly as it is linked to sexual hedonism.

Madonna embodies a social construction of "whiteness" that emphasizes purity, pure form. Indeed her willingness to assume the Marilyn Monroe persona affirms her investment in a cultural vision of white that is tied to imperialism and colonial domination. The conquest of light over dark replays the drama of white supremacist domination of the Native American, African, etc. In that representation of whiteness, Dyer asserts, "being white is coterminous with the endless plenitude of human diversity." He explains: "If we are to see the historical, cultural, and political implications (to put it mildly) of white world domination, it is important to see similarities, typicalities within the seemingly infinite variety of white representation." At the start of her career, the "whiteness" that Madonna flaunted was represented as other than, different from the mainstream, more connected to the reality of folks marginalized by race or sexual practice. For a time, Madonna seemed to desire to occupy both that space of whiteness that is different and the space that is familiar. Different, she is the young Italian white girl wanting to be black. Familiar, she is Marilyn Monroe, the ultimate cultural icon of white female beauty, purity, and sensuality.

Increasingly, Madonna occupies the space of the white cultural imperialist, taking on the mantle of the white colonial adventurer moving into the wilderness of black culture (gay and straight), of white gay sub-culture. Within these new and different realms of experience she never divests herself of white privilege. She maintains both the purity of her representation and her dominance. This is especially evident in *Sex*. In stories of sexual adventures told in *Sex*, people of color appear as primary protagonists. In one, the young Puerto Rican boy virgin is the "object" of the fictive Dita/Madonna's lust. We are told: "He was fearless. He would do anything...I was so turned on; it was probably the most erotic sex I ever had. But he gave me crabs." The stereotypes here are obvious, a fact which makes them no less damaging. Madonna's text constructs a narrative of pure white womanhood contaminated by contact with the colored "other." It would be easy to dismiss this construction as merely playful if it were not so consistent throughout *Sex*. In another adventure story an apparently well-off white male enters a fancy department store where he is sexually seduced by a Cuban salesgirl. She is, of course, as stereotype would have it, hot and whorish, ready to cheat on her boyfriend when any anonymous "desiring" white man looks her way. The structure of this narrative suggests that it, like the previous one, appeals directly to white supremacist sexual fantasies.

Though *Sex* appears to be culturally diverse, people of color are strategically located, always and only in a subordinate position. Our images and culture appear always in a context that mirrors racist hierarchies. We are always present to serve white desire. And while *Sex* exploits the myth of jungle fever, Madonna is carefully positioned within a visual framework where the big black man and the black woman appear as a couple who are her sexual servants; no readers could imagine that Madonna is partnering herself with a black male. No, all her images of conventional heterosexual coupling are with "nice" white boys. Black female sexuality is stereotypically represented as degraded. In the much-remarked and visually powerful come shot, Madonna stands over the prostrate naked body of black female model Naomi Campbell (not an anonymous fantasy image) and mimics a golden shower, by squirting lotion on the reclining figure. This image conveys a serious visual message about race, gender, and nationality. Madonna can be seen here as representing the imperialism of the United States, its triumph over Britain (Campbell is British Caribbean) as well as the conquest of "exotic" black cultures. Campbell has been called by white dominated fashion media the new Josephine Baker, a persona which directly contrasts that of idealized white womanhood. As the celebrated "primitive" icon, she must learn her place in relation to the white mistress and master. To conquer and subordinate this representation of "wild black sexuality," Madonna must occupy a phallic position. In keeping with sexist/racist iconography, the black female is symbolically subordinated by white male power; in this case it is Madonna assuming the white supremacist patriarchal role.

Throughout *Sex*, Madonna appears as the white imperialist wielding patriarchal power to assert control over the realm of sexual difference. None of this is mitigated by the recognition—emphasized by Madonna herself—that gender is an act of social construction. Nor can Madonna's disguises, however richly layered, ultimately mask her violence and cruelty towards women. Discussing gender parity, Carol-Anne Tyler ("Boys Will Be Girls: The Politics of Gay Drag") suggests that the male drag queen's femininity is "a put on, not the real thing, signaling he has what women like, the phallus." Though Madonna, of course, cannot do male drag, she does appropriate a drag queen look or style. Tyler identifies this female impersonator of the male impersonator as a phallic mother, insisting that "when the active desiring woman still reflects man's desires, the mirrors of the patriarchal imagination cannot have been shattered." In Madonna's latest persona as phallic mother she lets us know that she has no desire to shatter patriarchy. She can occupy the space of phallocentrism, be the patriarch, even as she appears to be the embodiment of idealized femininity.

She claims not to envy men, asserting: "I wouldn't want a penis. It would be like having a third leg. It would seem like a contraption that would get in the way. I think I have a dick in my brain. I don't need to have one between my legs." No doubt that "dick" in her brain accounts for Madonna's inability to grasp that feminism, or for that matter, women's liberation, was never about trying to gain the right to be dicks in drag. But wait a minute, I seem to recall that the men I knew back when the contemporary feminist movement was "hot" all believed that us little women didn't really want our freedom, we just wanted to be one of the boys. And in fact those same men, no doubt thinking through the dicks in their brains, told us that if we "women libbers" just had a good fuck, we would all come to our senses and forget all about liberation. We would in fact learn to find pleasure in being dominated. And when feminists did not fall for this dick rap, men tried to seduce us into believing with our brains and our bodies that the ultimate power was to be found in being able to choose to dominate or be dominated. Well, many of us said "thank you but no thanks." And some of us, well, some of us were tempted and began to think that if we could not really have our freedom then the next best thing would be to have the right to be dicks in drag, phallocentric girls doing everything the boys do—only better.

This gaslighting seductive message has so seduced

Madonna that now she can share the same phallic rap with her feminist sisters and all her other fans. Most of the recent images she projects in videos, films, photographs, etc. tell women and everyone that the thrill, the big orgasm, the real freedom is having the power to choose to dominate or be dominated. This is the message of *Sex*.

Madonna's feminist fans, once so adoring, are on the positive tip when we insist that we want an end to domination, when we resist her allure by saying no—no more seduction and betrayal. We long for the return of the feminist Madonna, the kind of cultural icon Susan Griffin celebrates in *Women and Nature* when she writes: "We heard of this woman who was out of control. We heard that she was led by her feelings. That her emotions were violent. That she was impetuous. That she violated tradition and overrode convention...We say we have listened to her voice asking, 'Of what materials can that heart be composed which can melt when insulted and instead of revolting at injustice, kiss the rod?'...And from what is dark and deep within us, we say, tyranny revolts us; we will not kiss the rod."

SUSIE BRIGHT

# A Pornographic Girl

Like most of the baby-boomer, thirty-something audience targeted for Madonna's *Sex*, I received a typical little girl education about sex, and it went something like this:

1) Girls don't know very much about sex, and they
   don't need to know more.
2) Girls need love, not sex.
3) Don't expect to come.

Men were typically described as inherently aggressive, naturally promiscuous and objectifying, exclusively genitally-focused; prone to sexual addictions, dangerous pornographic masturbation, and in general, needing to be contained so that their active pursuit of sexuality wouldn't be a public menace.

Women were lauded for our inherently sexual gentility and monogamous nature, equating our desire with romantic love, our sex with a nurturing non-genitally focused sensuality. Sexual pleasure and liberation were absolutely not priorities for women. Finally, women never used, produced or enjoyed pornography.

And if you believe any of the above, I've got a great little piece of property to show you on Love Canal...

The early women's liberation movement threw these notions in the trash, and sooner than you could say "eat my clit," women were revealing their sexual appetites in unprecedented numbers. In a vulva-shaped nutshell, the message was find your clit, learn to create your orgasm, express your sexual curiosity to its fullest, and don't let anyone, especially any man, tell you how to get off.

During my years as a sex activist, introducing women to the words that describe our sexual lives, to the pictures of our bodies and desires, to the confidence of hearing other women's common and kinky sexual experiences—well, there's been no turning back. Sexually, there is nothing new under the sun. But there are still so many shadows, and it has been the talking and writing and revealing that have cast us into the light.

So what's so bad about *Sex* ?

Thousands of people have a ready answer, thousands who have never touched the Mylar bag o'erotica that pop celebrity Madonna has fashioned to illustrate her sexual fantasies. The indignant consumer sounds the battle cry: "I will not buy this book. I REFUSE."

It is a particularly American outrage, and it begins with a presumably penny-pinching reproach: This book costs too much. Who would pay fifty dollars for a book? The kind of people who pay fifty dollars for a book are the very group who were trashing *Sex* as they left Zuni Café last night with a sixty dollar margarita bill; they're the ones who sniff at the idea of erotica but who spent forty dollars on cat calendars last year at A Clean Well Lighted Place; they're the people who didn't buy a hardcover book all year, but Nintendo owns their MasterCard.

Face it, the market for Madonna's book was never intended to be teenagers with lousy allowances or the unemployed monitoring their January heating bill. This is a book for yuppies, for art book fanciers and erotica enthusiasts, all of whom are known to blow money on items both extremely personal and of questionable taste.

The other reason for not buying *Sex* is celebrity nausea. You gagged on Hillary Clinton's cookies, you don't give a damn if Drew Barrymore crawls into a pile of cocaine and never climbs out, and if one more adult child of Ronald Reagan writes an autobiography you are going to hurl. There's something to be said for the ennui and exasperation we feel when fifteen-minute celebrities publish the meager facts of their lives.

But with Madonna, the subject at hand elicits something a little bit closer to envy—many of us wouldn't mind having a budget to illustrate our sexual imaginations. Some artists are in a state of shock over the news that Madonna has taken the substance of their cutting-edge erotic *tour de force* and turned it into profitable shelf space at Crown Books. I sympathize with the unheralded sex pioneers, because they're my comrades. But we are not any different than some Harlem vogue diva watching MTV with his mouth hanging open at Madonna's Hollywoodization of his original achievement.

That the book may be a rip-off, either financial or artistic, does not account for the bile that comes from the lips of the media and man-on-the street critics. What is hated about *Sex* is that it is "tawdry," "adolescent," "violent," and "kinky." Stripped of those pejoratives, the criticism is in essence an attack on the book's single-minded sexual premise. It is prima facie SEX, and hold onto your Kinsey Institute report, because sexual fantasies, whether Madonna's or anyone else's, are based on taboos, infantile (not to mention adolescent) memories, and repressed desires, which are often similar in sensation to fear and anger. Welcome to the world of the sexual unconscious.

The reputable side of erotica is tenderness and sensuality, a rapport between flesh and nature. This is well-represented in Madonna's book. She is a love child, just a skip away from flower power. Many of her images are filled with romance, gentleness, and humor—in fact, those pictures are the most affecting images in the book. Madonna applying lipstick to her boy lover's lips is more poignant in its delicacy than any shock from its gender-bending insinuations. Madonna's face on a pillow in the dark, her thumb to her mouth and eyes beginning to tear, evokes a lonely ache and yearning that is undeniable. Then there's Madonna's famous crotch, her mound of Venus arched in a beach ball spray of water, her dark pubic hair so luscious and different from her blond wigginess.

In vanilla, Madonna is at her best, at least through Meisel's approximation. In total though, Madonna takes on the *Penthouse Letters* portfolio of fantasies; every naughty thought on America's mind: black/white relations, Daddy's little girl, older seductress, cross-dressing, group sex, doggie sex, exhibitionism, and nonspecific wantonness. Her take on it all is not original; her photographer's eye is not transcendent.

Yet the images are still provocative, still have the power to affect us, simply because they are her Genuine Article and we, the audience, are completely unaccustomed to anyone being straightforward about what they like in bed.

Let's be candid. The reason there's a public outcry about *Sex* is that Americans don't think sex should be discussed in the light of day. Look at the polls on homosexuality. When it comes to what you do when the lights are out, no one gives a damn. A clandestine act of sodomy is far, far preferable to two men kissing in the park.

Americans, and our puritanical ancestors, the British, love nothing so much as to put down sex for being sexual. Nothing elevates one's standing like a careful arch quote that rains on the erotic parade. It's ever so clever to say what you don't like and completely outré to say what you do.

The biggest, most profound problem with Madonna's sexual encyclopedia (aside from the wretched binding job) is that it was produced with a set of instructions straight from the censor's little black book. Madonna was given the green light from Warner as long as she refrained from including pictures with penetration, explicit genitalia, sex with animals, and sex with children. This is a laundry list accepted by every legitimate publisher in the country, but what kind of sense does it make? What on earth do these four no-nos have to do with each other?

Madonna's writing is far more revealing than the photographs. We learn from her "diary entries" that she is a typical red-blooded American girl. She likes getting her pussy licked almost better than anything, she manipulates her clitoris when being fucked to reach an orgasm, and the only position she takes a hands-off approach to is on top. She likes to wake up and feel her lover's erection at her back. She's not fond of blow jobs but she's impressed to see one expertly performed. She speaks as highly of masturbation as Shere Hite. She is not ashamed of her genitals and she treasures her pussy as a source of life and pleasure.

Nevertheless, none of this basic introduction to women's sexual liberation is illustrated in her book. We never see Madonna masturbate or have intercourse, let alone reach orgasm. We never witness any of the models making the kinds of faces that reveal sexual ecstasy, because frankly they're never doing anything that would make them lose control.

Instead of going all the way, we get kinky foreplay. The most controversial photos in *Sex* are sadomasochistic. Her accompanying words are vulnerable and thoughtful about this notoriously misunderstood topic. But the pictures are as static as a Velcro release on a leather sling. S/M erotica in this country is nay style whipping—this is considered R-rated and acceptable. The line you cannot cross is to combine genital sexuality with these same images—this will force the artist/producer into an underground and illegal oblivion. To the uninitiated, this means that S/M in Madonna's book and elsewhere looks like a blackened kitchen demonstration. It's completely diabolical. If the point in getting spanked is to get off, then why do we never see the getting-off part?

Somebody, and I hope it will be a star with Madonna's power, needs to make a break with the standard obscenity code in this country, which insists that the most elemental (not to mention vanilla) sexual acts cannot be depicted because they are too dirty. If there's nothing disgusting about a woman's vulva, then why can't we see a picture of it without pornographic accusations? If making love is where love and ecstasy and babies come from, then what kind of absurd, hateful laws do we tolerate that forbid its artistic portrayal?

Madonna searched desperately for a printer in the United States. One finally came through but did not allow its name to be used in connection with the book. It tickled me to see that even Miss Invincible was faced with the problem every two-bit pornographer faces: no one turns on their press for dirty pictures. The commercial pornography industry survives in this country only because it bought its own printing plants.

Madonna, in the same spirit, has "bought" the right to publish a book like this. The wealthy have always had the ultimate access to freedom of speech, but few of them have stuck their necks out as she has. What is missing from all the tirades about Madonna's mediocrity is the fact that this book is by far her most serious work to date, both in its execution and its confrontation with the status quo. Her songs are tunes with a good beat that you can dance to (despite some academic attempts to deconstruct otherwise). Her movie appearances have been embarrassing a good eighty percent of the time. Her politics, though, are her most original strength. She possesses the outspoken feminist idealism and compassionate philanthropy that made liberal heroines out of Susan Sarandon, Whoopi Goldberg, and Jane Fonda. The popularity they enjoy with the politically correct eludes Madonna for one reason only: she is a "sex maniac." And being a very public and willing sex maniac is the most original, radical, and courageous thing that Madonna Ciccone has ever done.

**SIMON FRITH**

# The Sound of *Erotica*: Pain, Power, and Pop

## Art

Madonna's genius is a matter of taste, not technique, and I've always supposed that this genius involved an element of luck. To begin with, she arrived in New York at just the right time. She became a pop diva in the wash of Debbie Harry, who had pioneered the craft of marketing the tough as the tender and turning thrift-store sex appeal into performance art. Madonna first appeared as a teen star and remains one, even now, despite the "adult" sales pitch. I would guess that the bulk of her record sales are to eight-to sixteen-year-old girls. Her success reflects Harry's most brilliant ploy: Madonna plays out the fantasies of the knowing big sister and the wannabe little sister simultaneously.

Even more importantly, Madonna hit New York at exactly the right club moment, when the city's dance music was in the midst of its glorious ride along the cusp of the mechanical and the soulful, when old r&b conventions of vocal dirt and desire were being deployed by a new generation of engineers who layered the dance floor's background noise with a percussive care, a sense of temporal order that turned even the most sweaty workout into an intellectual exercise.

*Erotica* is, then, Madonna's New York album. Ten of its fourteen tracks were produced by Shep Pettibone, king of the New York remix. Pettibone's skill was (and is) to open out the rhythmic implications of soul singing without denying either the strength or the vulnerability of the sound that he thus deconstructed. In one way this was to follow the logic of Eurodisco (the shared inspiration being Giorgio Moroder's work with Donna Summer) but Pettibone's best work (always with female singers) was much more insinuating. His respect for the voice meant that the relation of producer and singer had its own sexual tension, its own musical sense of the erotics of resistance and submission.

So Madonna's choice of Pettibone as musical partner on her current sexual journey makes perfect sense—her taste is impeccable. The problem Pettibone had to face was technical: Madonna is not the best kind of singer for this kind of sound. The dynamic of those early Salsoul records, the appeal of a New York studio singer like Sharon Redd, derived from a sense of power—of emotion—barely contained, the voice swelling demandingly around the beat, the singer pulling herself together again each time the producer broke her lines up into a tumble of urgent fragments.

By disco standards, Madonna's voice is a thin instrument. There's not much body in it; her vocal chords don't, in themselves, make enough noise to defy a rhythm track. She gets her effects not by switching gear but by switching register, and, whether she's singing from mouth or throat or chest, when she pushes her voice it becomes shrill and slightly petulant. Such technical failures needn't matter to a producer of Pettibone's skill, of course; it's not difficult to fake vocal feeling. But the impact of the mixes depends on their dramatization of a real struggle. He needs a sound to work against.

This raises another problem: as a star, Madonna has to be heard to be in charge, which is to deny the logic of the form. The essence of the New York disco sound was the anonymity of its voices, its abstraction of desire. Just as with the Brill Building pop of a previous New York era, the sex appeal of New York dance music lay in its aural enactment of its emotional narratives. These dance records were all ballads of sexual dependency, and their emotional effect was pointed up by the studio reality of the singers' musical dependency. The more powerful the disco diva, the more heart-stopping her vulnerability to producer trickery; New York disco meant assertion of control in situations—love, sex, and in the studio—in which singers had none.

Madonna is a control freak. She can't be vulnerable this way; she can't be anonymous. Not because she's a superstar, but because, musically, she has to be the center of attention (which is why she's a superstar). The consequence is obvious here just in mixing terms. Her voice is too far forward, it blocks out those wisps of sound, those lurking riffs that on the dance floor should be the object of anxiety and anticipation. *Erotica*, like most Madonna albums, will work best as a series of twelve-inch remixes; as it is, each track goes on a little too long, each situation is played out before the music stops.

There's a paradox here, which Madonna understands: it is because she must be in musical control that she can only sing with a sense of caution. If the classic disco singer was held in by her producer, Madonna holds herself back and in doing so also holds back the rhythm—all the music here has a drag on it. The problem is most obvious on her version of "Fever": any sense of passion is flattened by the nervous care Madonna devotes to the articulation of the words.

If "Fever" is a failure, Madonna is otherwise a shrewd enough musician to work her limitations, and *Erotica* is Madonna's best record if only for its display of an unusual pop intelligence. Her most obvious solution to her lack of vocal range is her constant shift of voice, but *Erotica* also showcases her distinctive ability as a songwriter. For all her musical stiffness, that is, she does swing. Her adroitness in writing lyrical lines that change their rhythmic structure as they unfold gives her voice the momentum that she can't cede to Pettibone's machines; her deftness in constructing melodic units out of conversational stress-points at least lets certain words and sounds float free.

## Sex

In the first of her various exclusive interviews, Madonna told *New Musical Express*'s Gavin Martin that there was no connection between the album *Erotica* and the book *Sex:* "The only way they're interlinked is that there's a CD in the book which is a remixed version of the title track on my album, and that's the only way that they have anything in common."

But Madonna records don't fall from the sky, and *Sex* (the pictures) has been central to the hype of *Erotica* (the songs). All Madonna records are sold as soundtracks to her life, this one is being sold as the soundtrack to her sex life. Sex as such only pops up on three numbers—"Erotica," an invitation to light S/M, "Where Life Begins," a treatment of cunnilingus as a religious rite, and "Did You Do It?," a pastiche of rap as male sexual display. But if there's nothing else so verbally direct (the remaining tracks are mostly love songs) the album's premise is still that this is sexy music.

The question, then, is whether music as music can be sexy. Isn't it, like sex, an empty sign? Isn't a melody or beat, like an orgasm, meaningless? Surely music, like sex, only takes on emotional significance by becoming part of a story, a narrative of need and power and desire. *Erotica* features desire and need and power all right, but how do we recognize sexual power, sexual desire, sexual need?

One of Madonna's current projects is clearly the *naming* of sex. As a political project—a counter to the refusal to name sex—this seems sensible enough, but as a philosophical task it has its problems. Both euphemism ("Where Life Begins" employs coy dining metaphors) and talking dirty ("Did You Do It?" shows up the emptiness of rude words) suggest the futility of attempting to possess in language what can't be possessed in the sex act itself—the *meaning* of the body.

An alternative is to get at sex through sounds. In musical practice this means not squelching noises but a conventionalized intimacy, a "sexy" voice, breathy, close to the ear. Sex is indicated by the breaks within the music, the hesitations, sighs, and silences; the speaking voice is sexier than the singing voice because it is not determined formally, by the music, but emotionally, by the body's own demands and ripples. Madonna's music is very sexy in these terms, but it speaks a particular kind of sexuality—sex as therapy.

Madonna has always related sexuality to health, treated sex as another way of working out. Her slogan—sex is *good* for you—seems less a call to self-indulgence than a call to self-improvement. The further implications of *Erotica*—sexual exercises framed by fantasy—is that sex is also necessary for mental health; it is a way of dealing with anxiety. If nothing else, Madonna takes sex very seriously. She invites us to worship at her vagina less as an object of pleasure than as a source of truth.

The argument is plain: Madonna is sex; Madonna music is sex music. But I doubt that music works like pornography, as a source of masturbation fantasy; imagine yourself as an object of Madonna's desires! Imagine her as an object of yours! Music's sexual charge is either as a soundtrack for one's own seductions or as a form of voyeurism, a spilling out of calls and sounds and movements normally only heard in the privacy of a lover's ear. The sexiest song on *Erotica* is the title track, which is posed as a direct come-on but feels like something overheard, a siren's call drifting through a car window, a sound at once tempting and futile.

## Pain

My favorite tracks on *Erotica* celebrate not sex but pop. "Deeper and Deeper" is the New York take on Stock Aitken Waterman, Madonna doing her Kylie Minogue number, a paean to swirling self-help. "Thief of Hearts" is a girl-group dialectic, the lines tripping over their own outrage. When it comes to romance Madonna is incurably adolescent. Her songs are about the unfair unbalance of love—I don't love him ("Bye Bye Baby"); he don't love me ("Waiting"). She takes for granted that the rest of the world is shaped by her feelings—"Words" (the downside of love) and "Rain" (the up) relentlessly use grand old teen imagery. She effectively sentimentalizes self-pity ("Bad Girl") and self love ("Secret Garden").

For its market niche, *Erotica* is just another Madonna album. It follows the formula that made her a fortune (and set the terms for all subsequent female idols). Lyrically, melodically, and emotionally it is teenage pop; vocally, rhythmically, and aurally it is sophisticated dance music. And there may be nothing more to say. Madonna and her crew know just what they are doing: why mess with success? But as she ups the stakes in self-exposure I can't help wondering whether Madonna's stardom, her remarkably sustained stardom, isn't an effect of something less calculated: her inability to grow up.

The recurring theme of Madonna interviews is that no one

will take her seriously. She stresses that the most important lesson she learned from her beloved dance teacher (mourned here on "In This Life"), and more recently from her analyst, is that she must stop "being afraid to be herself." This combination of self-assertion and self-doubt has always been the essence of her appeal, but it takes on a new pathos in the context of Madonna as sex therapist. And it's easy enough for pop psychologists to finger Madonna's problem; only when feeling completely in command can she dare to risk abandon. Hence her interest in sadomasochism, the simulacrum of submission.

*Erotica* opens with Madonna's offer to inflict a little punishment, but mostly concerns emotional pain, the effect of letting lovers into one's life without ties. She never makes us believe, though, that anyone is really hurt. And in this respect, much as I admire Madonna's musical taste and intelligence, she's not a great pop singer. She doesn't reach the melodic edge; her voice is too restricted. It's not simply that when it comes down to it "pain" is what Madonna inflicts upon herself routinely, in the pursuit of health and efficiency (unlike the great pop singers, she lacks all signs of sluttishness). It's also that she won't take the musical chances that might open her up to ridicule (and singing is, by its nature, embarrassing). As usual I end up admiring a Madonna album but not being touched by it; as usual the fascination is not what Madonna reveals but how she's been dressed up.

DOUGLAS CRIMP AND MICHAEL WARNER

# No Sex in *Sex*

## 1. Appropriation is a weird term

DC: Let's begin with why we don't think *Sex* is queer enough. Like everything Madonna does, you can say it's good because…, it's bad because…. So, it's good because it's queer, but still it's not satisfying. Is this because, in the end, it's all Madonna, so we feel that she's stolen something from us?

MW: Do you think we'd inevitably feel that way, no matter what the images were like?

DC: My reaction to *Sex* is similar to my reaction to the "Justify My Love" video, where the catalogue of perversions— voyeurism, lesbianism, transvestitism, S/M—plays a very standard role, as prelude to "real" sex, as foreplay. It's meant to titillate Madonna's then-boyfriend Tony Ward.

MW: And it came packaged in a narrative setting where all of this happens inside a room in a dingy hotel that Madonna has gone to. The camera shows her going into the room in the beginning and leaving it at the end, and that frames it as safely somewhere else. She's done the same thing in *Sex*. In the pictures taken at the Gaiety, she's wearing an evening gown and feather boa and she's escorted by two men in tuxedos. She's out for an evening on the town; she's a tourist in this strange little place that's buried away somewhere. So let's get back to your question about why this isn't queer enough. The scenes with Allistair Fate and Julie Tolentino, are they not queer enough?

DC: We'd have to ask lesbians. But I think the queerness is compromised by the supposed hilarity. Madonna says of these pictures that they're meant to be a joke—as in, "lesbianism is a joke." And everyone—from the most straight laced critics to Camille Paglia—refers to the two women as "those lesbian skinhead freaks." So the turn-on is that it's freaky.

MW: Or turn-off, depending on your taste. Paglia obviously perceives Julie and Allistair as the sort of people who don't like her, so she claims that these are the worst pictures. People typically project something about their own tastes in their supposed analyses of formal content. Paglia thinks that the photographs that show Madonna straddling things are great pictures!

DC: But that's always a problem in writing about sex. No matter how theoretical or objective you think you're being, it seems you're condemned to write about your own sexual proclivities, tastes, and desires, and to find everyone else's incomprehensible or boring or strange or wrong.

MW: It's not so hard to write about pornography if you find it stimulating. The difficult thing is to write about the porn that you don't get aroused by and still treat it as pornography, even successful pornography.

DC: But almost no one seems to see this book as successful, as a turn-on.

MW: It's true, the people I've talked to who've liked *Sex* have liked it for its humor or for its educational value, not because it's a turn-on. People think the book brings queers into public visibility.

DC: Do you think that our ability to recognize the skinhead guys as queer is generally shared?

MW: I don't know. One of the pictures with them is the "rape picture," and I've heard a lot of people complain about it. But to me it's made ridiculous because the men are so obviously queer, so I read it as a parodic reference to a rape narrative rather than an arousing simulation of one.

DC: In fact, anyone with any sense can see that they're queer, because they're French kissing each other two pages before.

MW: Yeah, you recognize them from the nipple rings. This is one of the things that bugs me about the queerness of the book. I get the feeling that all these queer guys are not doing what they want to do. They're being told, "OK, stand here, do this to Madonna." And you know this because you know people like this and you know what it's like to have sex with them. They have certain desires and tastes, and those desires and tastes are not being reflected here; they're being shoved aside so that the guys can serve as signifiers of something else.

DC: The people are recognizable as queer, some of the acts that Madonna is performing are recognizable as queer—acts like rimming—but it still feels like an appropriation.

MW: Appropriation is a weird term, though, because in a way you always win these battles by being appropriated. If you're going to conquer cultural turf and gain a certain amount of legitimacy, how else is it going to happen except through the appropriation of certain rhetorics by people who haven't hitherto been part of the minority culture? The term may be the sign of an inevitable ambivalence.

DC: The reason I use the term is because Time-Warner would never do this for someone identified as gay. Everything about this is made possible by Madonna's celebrity, and her celebrity is constructed, in however complex a way, as *heterosexual*. She can be as queer as she wants to, but only because we know she's not.

MW: If we tried to do this we'd have trouble finding a printer to produce the book. In fact, the printer who did *Sex* previously refused to print gay books, including Alyson Publications's *Gay Sex*. Even if we could find a printer, we wouldn't be able to persuade bookstores to carry it or *Vanity Fair* to review it, even badly. So, as you say, the whole production and reception of the book is already framed by our absence from it.

DC: So our dissatisfaction comes down to something as simple as self-determination, of queers being allowed to have our own voices.

MW: I think we could go farther; Madonna is not unwilling to treat queers as strange and even a little disgusting.

DC: Yeah, the last of the "Dear John" letters, where Dita responds to having discovered John and Ben having sex together, is really homophobic. She writes, "As for me, I think I'm going to be sick. Next time you want pussy, just look in the mirror."

MW: It's both homophobic and misogynist. In *Body of Evidence* Madonna allows herself to play a character with the same attitude in exactly the same situation. The movie has one of the most homophobic scenes to come out of Hollywood for a long time: Madonna tells a courtroom that she found her boyfriend in bed with another man. "I couldn't compete!" she wails, tragically, and she literally shames the man out of the courtroom.

DC: Then again, if you try to read *Sex* for political correctness, you're in big trouble. Like the text about the Puerto Rican boy who gives her crabs. Can Madonna really be unaware of the stereotype of the filthy spic? I guess the fact that she begins with the kid's virginity and ends with "But he gave me crabs" is supposed to be funny.

MW: You think that was deliberate? She seems to have total amnesia from one sentence to the next. Her race fantasies seem conventional and unreflective to me, as in the Oreo cookie with Naomi Campbell, Madonna, and Big Daddy Kane. The thing that people say to redeem her is that she's relatively open to queer sexuality, but I'm not sure that she is. The gay men in the book seem to be there more as suppliers of sexual glamour than as actual sexual partners, either with her or with each other. It's significant that the gay men in the book are either like Udo Keir—they keep their clothes on and look louche and exotic and show us how "interesting" faggots can be—or they're the Gaiety dancers; they're on display rather than acting out anything sexual. They're on a stage, they're framed by the theatrical apparatus of the club. It's more about their exotic appeal for a spectator than it is about gay sex.

DC: I think that's how the whole book works. "Sex" is a misnomer because what we get is just a show—a mild, softcore come-on.

MW: We're running up against the limits of our own vocabulary for talking about these things. Queer theory has insisted that sex and performance, desire and image, fantasy and narrative, and so on cannot be distinguished; yet when we try to talk about what we think is limiting or puzzling about *Sex*, we find ourselves trying to invoke the very distinctions that theory has been doing away with for the past fifteen years. So you have to invent a new vocabulary. Talk about queer performativity, *Sex* is nothing if not queer performativity, but that somehow doesn't make it queer enough; it doesn't make it sex.

## 2. Maybe we should ask Tipper Gore what she thinks

DC: There's something else I think we should consider. There were two predictable responses to the book: the bored response and the shocked response.

MW: The shocked response was anticipated by the publicity.

DC: Yes, the shocked one was what the book was going for, and you could almost say the book was a failure because it didn't elicit enough outrage. But I'm interested in the fact that we haven't heard a word about this book from the expected voices on the right. Where is Donald Wildmon? Where is Lou Sheldon? Where is Jesse Helms? Where is Pat Buchanan? One would think this book would be for those people as repulsively homoerotic as Robert Mapplethorpe's photographs or Marlon Riggs's videos or Holly Hughes's performances. Have the right-wing zealots kept quiet because they're smart enough to know to attack only those who are vulnerable, those who don't have Time-Warner behind them? Or is it because Madonna's presence sufficiently heterosexualizes it, or degays it?

MW: How would this book have been received differently if Bush had won the election? It came out at a point when the family-values people had obviously lost.

DC: There's something to that. If the climate in which this book was produced had been maintained by Bush's reelection, the book would have seemed more transgressive. People might not have been so quick to say, "This is banal." They might have said, "It's courageous." Of course, we shouldn't be too quick to assume that because Clinton won the election, things are going to be different on this front. Maybe we should ask Tipper Gore what she thinks of *Sex*. I really do find this interesting: Madonna's constituency is, for the most part, young. Really young. Teenagers. And presumably a lot of them are getting their hands on this book, and many more will do so when the cheap edition comes out. Why haven't we heard an outcry about this? Why haven't parents decided to boycott Time-Warner?

MW: Especially when they're going after the Rainbow Curriculum, which is much tamer than *Sex*.

DC: To say the least.

MW: You mentioned the possibility that the right perceives the book—correctly, I think the implication was—as fundamentally heterosexual and tame. I'm skeptical about that.

DC: You're right, sex is just sex for those people—and it's all bad.

MW: And they're stupid. They flew off the handle about Mapplethorpe, though we would say that from a certain point of view the Mapplethorpe images are also tame at best, if not aesthetically conservative and racist. That didn't stop them from protesting Mapplethorpe, so why has it stopped them from protesting *Sex?* It can't be because they've just lost with Bush and they think they have no more power. They do, obviously.

DC: And their cultural power is based on attacking things like this.

MW: Exactly. Having lost the election would be stimulus for them to attack *Sex*, so as to recover some of the ground they've lost. Maybe they're satisfied with the reviewers' discourse about its boringness. Maybe they figure that trashes the book better than they could do. But I don't think they're that smart, do you?

DC: All I can figure is that they know enough about power to know that they could be made to look ridiculous.

MW: That doesn't seem to be a possibility that Jesse Helms has ever contemplated before. And there is clearly a Madonna backlash going on now in the mass media. You would think that they would, like sharks, smell blood, and attack now. Because she is weak, she is vulnerable, just as Sinead O'Connor is now.

### 3. There are so many dangers of being ridiculous here

DC: In the end it's also why I've felt reluctant to respond to *Sex*—the whole thing has fallen flat. Although it has stayed on the bestseller list.

MW: In fact, consumers are rarely in sync with the press. It's like the myth of Reagan's popularity. For years the press has been saying that Reagan was the Great Communicator and the most popular president, while every poll has shown that he was no more popular than Carter. The press talks about how boring and uninteresting *Sex* is, while it sells every copy they can crank out, at fifty bucks a pop, and is in every store window—in those places where you *can* even get your hands on a copy.

DC: One of the reasons everyone says *Sex* is banal is that there's a terror of being banal oneself, of not being hipper than the book. As if everyone's sexual fantasies were so extraordinary.

MW: That shows up in Mim Udovich's *Voice* piece: she reports a friend's saying that everyone keeps telling him that *Sex* is boring, and he says, "I don't know, they must have more interesting lives than I do."

DC: My hesitancy to participate in the "Madonna studies" phenomenon is that I generally think and write about things that really do matter to me, and Madonna doesn't matter to me that much. But it's a problem even to say that, because it sounds like denial or snobbishness or elitism. At some point you have to ask, How can anything that's captured so many people's imaginations, that's generated so many millions of dollars, how can it fail to interest you? But then you get trapped into something like: how can it interest me differently? How can it interest me in a way that it doesn't interest other people? How can I have something original to say? There's the sense that this is a game you can't win, so then you have to examine why it is that you have to win in the first place. Why do you have to be the one who finally says something really interesting about Madonna?

MW: Yeah, we're confronted with the limits of our own cultural capital here. We can't allow ourselves just to be Madonna consumers because that's not what intellectuals do.

DC: But I suppose, finally, that's what I am. I'm a somewhat reluctant Madonna consumer. I listen to her songs in the bars, occasionally watch her videos on MTV, go see *Truth or Dare*.

MW: The only things I've ever really liked of Madonna's were the "Vogue" video and *Truth or Dare*—now we're sinking to the level of pure subjectivism, but of course we're doing so in order to reflect on it.

DC: Yeah, right.

MW: The first time I saw the "Vogue" video, I was in a gay club with a big video screen, and I felt like I'd died and gone to heaven, but not because of Madonna, because of the gay men. I couldn't believe a gay male practice was getting such explicit representation in a mass cultural form. What I loved about *Truth or Dare* was the way it was playing into the cultural battles over censorship at the time. It seemed to me an important response to the then-ascendant rhetoric of PC and family values and so on. Which again had little to do with Madonna herself or her music—I don't think she's anything of a musician.

DC: The first time I heard "Vogue" was one night at the Latino drag club La Escuelita, where it was lip-synched by Pepper Labeja, accompanied by two wonderful voguers. One of them was plump and sort of femme and the other one was sinewy and angular, very butch—he had had very extreme surgery and his chest and stomach were a mass of gorgeous scars. The first was pure fluidity and the other's movement was totally geometric. As a pair they were amazing because of the contrast of performance styles. But then, of course, "Vogue" became a vehicle for the truly ridiculous: white yuppies in clubs trying to vogue.

MW: There are just so many dangers of being ridiculous here. I think about what I just said about my response not having anything to do with Madonna, and of course it must have had to do with her. My pleasure in *Truth or Dare*'s talking back to the conservatives must have had something to do with the fact that Madonna was doing the talking. It's the point in the culture from which Jesse Helms would least expect resistance—a blonde from Michigan who sings clichés about love. How harmless can you be? So the fact that this was the point from which talking back was happening was an important aspect of the satisfaction. And with the "Vogue" video, the fact that so much of the visual rhetoric comes from advertising photography, which we've always known to be queer—the photographers are queer, the models are queer—but was never acknowledged as such. To see that rhetoric being deployed to acknowledge the black gay male practice of voguing was an added part of the satisfaction.

DC: But again you come up against the question I asked before about *Sex* and the right. Why can she get away with it? Why can she talk back in *Truth or Dare*, when a truly articulate voice about black queer sexuality such as Marlon Riggs's is silenced? Maybe the disappointment that people inarticulately express by saying this book is boring, or that the sexual fantasies are banal, is that it's a lost opportunity: Madonna has all that power behind her, she could have done something really transgressive. But then why would we expect Madonna, of all people, to do that? Her stock in trade is banality.

MW: There also seems to be a built-in disappointment or a built-in ambivalence in the idea of a mass-cultural icon for queers. Alice Echols said in her *Advocate* piece that it was a big shift in lesbian culture when lesbians started carrying placards of Madonna and Sandra Bernhard, since the idea of a lesbian icon had been anathema—I don't know how true this is—to an earlier generation that insisted on referring to Holly Near as a cultural worker rather than as a star. There's something weird in the idea of a star for lesbians or a mass-cultural icon for queers. We want to have such a thing, but we're going to have a certain amount of aggression toward anyone who occupies that position.

DC: It's difficult to know, because you can only fantasize the possibility. The construction of celebrity is still so homophobic.

MW: When there starts to be a bit of explicit discussion about the queerness of the icon, our contradictory wishes come into view—the wish that Madonna be queer, and the wish that

Madonna be an image of acceptability, life, and realism. These are preposterous demands at some point, but we want Madonna to provide access to queer legitimacy.

DC: What makes Madonna interesting to think about as a queer icon is that she inhabits the role in two different ways. On one hand, she is playing at being a lesbian. On the other hand, she is a camp star for gay men. She's bridging an otherwise unbridged gap between lesbian culture and gay male culture.

MW: Would it have been possible for any man to have bridged the gap?

DC: If you try to imagine a man doing this, first of all you have to decide if he's going to be straight or queer. If he were straight man he couldn't do anything queer. This is a latitude Madonna has that no straight man would have had. It's possible for a woman, especially a straight woman, to glamorize gay male sex without tainting herself. A straight man would find that hard to do.

MW: Do we think it's impossible just because no one has done it?

## 4. Michael Jackson's *Sex*

DC: Before we began this discussion, you suggested trying to think about how we would do such a book if we had the opportunity. How would it be different? Another possibility is to imagine how other celebrities might do it. Like, Michael Jackson's *Sex*. Wouldn't you like to have access to *his* fantasy life!

MW: That's a great idea, much more intriguing. Because there seems to be much more distance between his fantasy life and his cultural circulation. I guess this is what drives us crazy about *Sex:* you just can't believe there would be that much convergence between Madonna as public icon and the way she produces her fantasy life, which is all about the public iconicity.

There's nothing resistant about the book. You want to encounter something limiting about the image in relation to yourself, some interiority of the people in the images that you don't
quite have access to, some impossible insertion of yourself into
the images. These images are already designed with us in mind,
and that's not what we want. We want to be told that we have
no business being here. Michael Jackson communicates that in
a way that seems richly erotic and queer.

DC: That reminds me of something else I thought about in relation to your question about how we might reimagine *Sex*. And
that is, how might we imagine *Sex* as *not* queer. If Madonna had
wanted to do a book that was truly heterosexual, it becomes impossible to imagine, for me at least—this might be a limitation
of my own subjectivity. Wasn't she in fact compelled to make it
queer?

MW: One thing she does by making it queer is avoid the head-on
confrontation with mainstream pornography. The leather, masturbation, queers, animals—all that stuff allows her to avoid
the *Playboy-Hustler* rhetoric, which she occasionally alludes to
but manages to distance herself from.

DC: I suppose Madonna is involved in a very queer world. She
didn't have to contrive this. It was just there for her. Her collaborators—the photographer, the designer, the stylist, the editor (let's not forget the brilliant editor!), all the people who put
the book together—presumably they're mostly queer. She certainly hangs out with queers enough to have adopted queer
style for herself.

MW: How different would it be if, for example, we had pictures
of Madonna making out with Marky Mark?

DC: Just another queer image. It's hard to come up with a good
heterosexual. Madonna pretends to be acknowledging polymorphous perversity, but in fact what she's done is very conventional. What I could imagine as interesting or innovative would

be to sexualize bodies that do not come straight from the fashion and advertising industries. The fixation on the perfect youthful body, the Marky Mark body, is so conventional. The pictures of Madonna with the older man are so predictable: only she is the object of desire; he is not in any sense made desirable. And the accompanying text is about how disgusted Madonna is by fat.

MW: That's such a stupid piece of writing; just on a sentence-by-sentence level the stupidity is manifest in the non-relation between one clause and another. It's the most disappointing moment in the book: although it's pointed to as one of the shocking images, it is, as you say, totally conventional, precisely in the asymmetry between her desirability and his non-desirability. It would have been better to eroticize him—for her to be clothed and him to be unclothed, for example. Look at this, they flash his business suit, they flash his fucking wedding ring!

DC: But this is the terrain of sexuality that is truly taboo in the commercial figuring of desire, because it just might not sell.

MW: Older people, people who don't conform to the body type. We should probably say that we're both bald and older than Marky Mark.

DC: Wherever Madonna talks about what turns her off, she includes baldness, which is interesting, because in the opening sequences of the book, both the lesbians and the gay men have shaved heads. I remember one of the trash TV reports on the book in which the commentator feigned shock at the bald heads, as if no one had ever thought of a bald head as sexy before.

MW: The premise of the book seems to be that sex and glamour are the same.

DC: Madonna claimed in *Vogue* magazine that having her fantasies photographed for *Sex* was comparable to what Cindy Sherman does in her photographs. But nothing could be more different.

MW: Different how? Suppose one of Madonna's pictures were captioned "Cindy Sherman, Untitled, 1992"?

DC: In fact, Sherman did show a series of photographs last year that might be thought of as her version of *Sex*. And interestingly enough, it was her first series in which she didn't use herself as model. Instead she used anatomical dolls, sex toys, and other props. But in spite of the obvious artificiality of these objects, Sherman was able to conjure sexual intensities, including terror, disgust, pathos. I guess when we complain that there's no sex in *Sex* what we mean is that there's no intensity, no excess, no danger...

MW: No ugliness. Even the S/M stuff in Sex seems hokey because there's never even the illusion of pain. Or power, for that matter.

DC: Nobody's *doing* anything. It's just the trappings—boutique S/M, Gianni Versace.

**5. It's impossible to ignore the propriety.**

MW: One thing almost all the reviewers complain about is that the men in *Sex* look bored, or they play ancillary roles. *Sex* makes remarkably little effort to eroticize male bodies. It doesn't even do so in the manner of the Marky Mark Calvin Klein ads, which are done by Herb Ritts (the photographer Madonna dumped for Meisel), which use the same mainstream advertising language, and which have provoked much more erotic cathexis, at least much more talk about erotic cathexis. All the response to *Sex* has been that it's boring, it isn't a turn-on. All the response to the Marky Mark ads has been, What a turn-on! So let's compare these images.

DC: Marky Mark is a boy and Madonna is a girl.

MW: But straight men's and women's responses to the Marky

Mark ads and Madonna's book have followed the same pattern. If the Marky Mark ads didn't appeal to straight men and the women who buy for them, they wouldn't be successful advertising.

DC: Is that true? I always assumed that these images of hunky men—from the first Bruce Weber Calvin Klein underwear ads to last summer's Silver Tab ads—were directed at gay men.

MW: But isn't the secret appeal of these ads that straight men, who wear most of these products, have a queer imaginary? Even if all their narratives about themselves are heterosexual, they like looking at these ads and at some level get confused between wanting to have Marky Mark's appeal and wanting to have Marky Mark. But these ads bare so much of their homo appeal that they're starting to encounter some problems. And that brings me back to the comparison between *Sex* and the Marky Mark ads. There's so much similarity between the two, but the responses are opposite. One difference between the two is that the eroticism and the queerness are acknowledged in *Sex* whereas in the Calvin Klein ads there's still a veneer of denial, a veneer of Marky Mark's heterosexuality, signified by the woman who appears in a couple of the ads, so the underwear is meant to augment hetero potency rather than to be a come-on.

DC: Are they then attractive to queers because we still hang on to the illusion that we can read something ostensibly straight as queer?

MW: I think so. On one hand, it's frustrating that the homoeroticism is unacknowledged. On the other hand, the fact that it's not acknowledged allows us to have a fantasy victory because we think we can see the heterosexual disavowal at work. It's a fantasy triumph where we discover their secret homosexuality. Which may be all delusion, but it's how homophobic disavowal crosses the triumphalist fantasy of seeing the secret queerness of everybody.

DC: Look at these pictures of Vanilla Ice. They've made him look ridiculous on purpose.

MW: How much sport can there be in that? And the pictures go on forever. There are several things to think about here. Why Vanilla Ice? Is he really meant to be erotic? Or why the choice of these positions, where it looks like he's trying to fuck Madonna from behind, except that he has his pants on? But then there are the other decisions, those of Meisel and Baron, such as the superimposed images and the color separations. Those decisions just look retarded to me.

DC: One of them makes Vanilla Ice appear to be wearing high heels.

MW: And it's hard to tell whose butt this is.

DC: Except it couldn't be his, because his is so flat.

MW: But if it's hers, then she's in the fucking position rather than the fucked position. Well, we're making it look a little less retarded. But how could the design and photography be as incompetent as they appear to be, given the price tag and the power of the advertising industry behind it?

DC: And the prestige of the people doing it.

MW: One of the most visually exciting moments in the book for me is that spread with Madonna, Allistair Fate, and Julie Tolentino, where you see the back of one of the girls' heads and the texture of the stubble is very clearly rendered. To me it's really erotic. Although it also has to be said that in this sequence of pictures, more than any other in the book, Madonna is perfectly coifed. She seems to have pancake makeup on to make her skin look more pallid than usual and thus to form more of a contrast to the lesbians. In this picture where she's got the "Oh-my-God-I-can't-believe-we're-doing-this" look on her face, her blond ringlets are perfectly arranged, her eyebrows are perfectly plucked and lined, her lipstick is perfectly laid on. It seems to be designed to mark her off from exactly the things I find appealing about the other girls in that scene.

DC: I guess you could read it as a kind of butch-femme scenario.

MW: I distrust that. Her clothing's wrong.

DC: Yeah, and there's no reason for two butches. I guess it's more like lesbians having sex together, with Madonna along for the ride.

MW: These pictures are moderately interesting, with the lesbians at the urinal and the gay men beside them. And this one, where she's shaving the guy's pubic hair with a ghostly image of the queers superimposed on it. But in that one I can't get over the prudishness in the way her hand is cupped so artfully over the guy's dick while she's shaving him. It's impossible to ignore the propriety of that image.

DC: Yes, well, there's only one dick in the whole book.

MW: And it's limp. You can imagine a rationale for that. You can either like or dislike the dicklessness of *Sex* and the choice will be determined by your choice between two different ways of characterizing the dominant culture. Either you say the absence of dicks in *Sex* is good because it rejects the dominant culture's insistence on male erection and sexuality as penetration; or you say it's bad because it's complicit with the culture's unwillingness to show erections as desirable objects.

DC: There would be an easy way to resolve it, especially since the one dick you see is at the Gaiety. You could have another man licking it, or holding it.

MW: Or even looking at it. Everyone else is turned away in that picture, especially Madonna. Even Udo Keir is looking the other way.

DC: Madonna writes so much about her pussy, it seems as if she really wants to get the focus off the cock. But does she manage to do that in a way that challenges the way we think about sex?

MW: I've talked to lesbians who really love those pages about her pussy—you know, "My pussy is the temple of learning."

DC: Isn't that a bit pretentious?

MW: Well, for overwriting, how about "that glorious day when finger found flesh and with legs spread open and back arched, honey poured from my 14-year-old-gash and I wept"? I think this is the sort of passage that Mim Udovitch had in mind when she described *Sex* as the true sequel to *Gone with the Wind*. Both of those passages are stilted and, in a way, ridiculous. But you can imagine giving yourself over to their ridiculousness in a pleasurable way. And you can imagine thinking that just to have someone say these things in public is progress.

DC: That's true. You could say that in a general way about the whole book, for two reasons. First, any form, no matter how compromised, of sex positivity in this cultural climate, you have to be happy about. It's fun to imagine the crew of *Sex* working at the time of the Republican convention. And second, it takes pride in female sexuality. These are the things people have valued about Madonna for some time.

MW: With these two pages about her pussy, though, it's even better: they're not heterosexual pages. There's not even a heterosexual fantasy legitimating them. It's total autoeroticism. And despite the pretentiousness of "My pussy is the temple of learning," there's something I like about it, too—the whole idea that your body is the scene of an ongoing education. One of the things denied in the chatter about the boringness of the book is that we have things to learn, still.

DC: Can we stop now? I'm bored.

JOHN CHAMPAGNE

# Stabat Madonna

*A meditation suggested by the work of that apologist for Christianity with the shapely calves.*

## I.

I was recently invited, along with several other gay and lesbian writers, to read at a large bookstore in a south suburb of Pittsburgh, a bookstore which, while not advertising itself as gay, lesbian, or even feminist, has often shown its support for these constituencies and communities by stocking books of interest to them, as well as maintaining a suburban funky intellectual atmosphere of liberal tolerance and inclusion. The event was organized specifically to celebrate Gay and Lesbian Pride Month, presenting a handful of local writers reading from their own works in progress.

The reading took place in a downstairs corner of the bookstore, where a number of chairs had been gathered cozily around a fireplace and podium. We were not supplied with a microphone, but we were still in earshot of much of the store's clientele, the majority of whom were clearly not in attendance specifically for the reading. Although I was nervous about the fact that I was reading for what could turn out to be a largely unreceptive, if not downright hostile, audience, I was comforted by the store's announcement, over the p.a. system, that this was in fact a reading organized to celebrate gay and lesbian pride. (I am accustomed to people walking out of my readings when I begin describing two men fucking, but I like to be prepared for this possibility.) Coincidentally, though not insignificantly, the reading took place within hearing distance of the children's section of the store, where a number of small children squealed impatiently as their parents looked through suitable reading material for them.

Perhaps it was the proximity of our event to the children's books that impelled at least two of the other writers to preface their work with the statement that, because this was a "family" bookstore, they would not be reading a great deal of their usual material, material which featured explicit representations of gay and lesbian sexuality. As I awaited my turn to read, I was reminded of Foucault's argument, in *Discipline and Punish*, that modern disciplinary society works to institute standards of normality not through the deployment of coercive displays of brute force, but by teaching subjects to maintain a vigilant form of self-surveillance. Such internalized surveillance is economical in that it requires a minimum expenditure of power in general, and state power in particular, to achieve a maximum result. Thus even at a reading which was organized specifically to celebrate gay and lesbian pride, our own sense of shame at being "abnormal," and in such close proximity to "innocent" families and children, made possible a kind of self-censorship which no oppressive state power "outside" of us needed to enforce directly. As Foucault reminds us, this is the hallmark of a successful disciplinary mechanism: the threat of detection alone is enough to ensure the continued production of docile, cooperative subjects.

I was scheduled to read at the very end of the program. When it came time for me to read, I invited my audience to look around the room to see if they could guess who would be the first to leave once I started reading about sex between men. I began by stating that since this was a family bookstore I would read a poem about having sex with married men:

THREE POEMS OF MARRIED MEN

*I. The Tailor*
Bourbon, warm milk, honey.
The sadness of afternoon.
"You have the hairiest ass
I have ever seen in my life."
Making love on the sewing room floor,

Sea of emerald moiré, cream tulle,
Scraps from an August wedding.
His wife was four months pregnant.
His hands, his hands, measuring the inseam
Of my sixteen years,
Years of waiting for some man
To do me this meager favor,
Years of just shut up and fuck me.
Against my back
The carpet burns.
Crying in the Buick.
In the shower, I come again.
His penis, like an animal in the zoo.
I fall asleep on the couch,
My fist pressed against my mouth.

*II. The Band Director*
In your yellow office,
You pull out your dick
As if I should be impressed.
At seventeen, I've already learned
What lies and a little contempt can manage.
I hear your children laughing,
Only a locked door divides
Their father on his knees
From a game of hide and seek.
Your face jerks wildly between my legs,
I'm pulling the string, puppet head.
When you tell me you love me,
I get up to brush my teeth.
In ten years, they will send you away
For fondling some child
In the middle of his trombone lesson.
In prison, you will discover Jesus,
Be born again as husband and father,
Return to your wife,
The woman you once told me you imagined as me
As you moved in and out of her.

### III. The Organist

My father circles the kitchen,
Anger gathered up in his hands
Like an ape, like a jealous lover
He sniffs my meager guilt.
"He slept on the sofa," I lie.
"Besides, he's getting a divorce."
Where did I learn such a steely deceit,
Who taught me its workings?
"The day he gets that divorce," my father swore,
"I'll stick the papers up my ass."
In the front seat of his car,
I come in his mouth,
He kisses it back into mine.
Is it a sin,
Have I finally committed an act
No god would know?
My grandma Ruth, five years dead,
Gave me a quarter for every beer I would bring her.
She is who I remember
As I swallow my own semen.
I tie a gold loop
Around his neck, promise
Too much at twenty.
Nine years and his forty pounds later,
He calls on my birthday, tells me
He's sent his wife and children to Europe,
Will I visit?
I ask him to spell his last name.
He reminds me of the size of his dick.

After the reading, someone in the audience congratulated those of us gathered specifically for the event on the fact that no one appeared to have left as a result of my work. This same "liberal" bookstore where we had gathered was perhaps not coincidentally featured on the local news recently as one of the few places in Pittsburgh which had ordered a significant number of copies of *Sex*.

Before even seeing Madonna's book, I had an argument concerning its merits (or lack thereof) with my mother (over the telephone, no less—since neither of my parents is university educated, they frequently indulge me in these attempts to perform, long distance, as a critic, and are not really in a position to challenge my sometimes overzealous and hasty assertions). My mother hadn't seen *Sex* either, but on the basis of what her friends said, she deemed it "trash"—a word she once applied to my own second novel. She informed me that everyone had reported that the book was foul, a sleazy attempt by a greedy media hound to cash in on her star persona by shocking people. I responded that if in fact everyone was trashing the book, it would be my duty as a critic to complicate this dominant reading of the text by finding what might be recuperable in it. My mother scoffed at the idea that anything worthwhile could come of *Sex*; I reminded her that while she and my father, being proper liberal sixties parents, had provided me with a fairly extensive education in what was then referred to as the facts of life, there was never any discussion among us of the clitoris. It was as if this organ didn't even exist. As usual in these kinds of discussions with my mother, this immediately plunged her into that never depleted, ever flowing reservoir of Catholic guilt which forced her to confess that, yes, she was not always the model parent. Not to be distracted from my point, I continued that owing to the prevalence of this continued cultural silence around female sexuality, it is important that a book like *Sex* be published, distributed, and discussed.

In one of the prose passages of *Sex*, Madonna writes, "I'm not interested in porn movies because everybody is ugly and faking it and it's just silly." Interestingly, this charge could in fact be leveled at much of *Sex*, which includes a number of not conventionally attractive people engaged in simulated sex in ways that often appear pretty silly. In the scenes depicting S/M activities in particular, she seems to have chosen her (simulated) sex partners from a virtual rogues' gallery. I realize that I am on shaky ground here. My attempt to name a particular image as erotically interesting is necessarily caught up in contradictory circumstances: on the one hand, what I find sexually arousing may not be so for others, and, on the other hand, like all of us, I have been positioned historically to find only a finite and perhaps limited number of representations to be erotically compelling. Nonetheless, I have to admit that I found the photograph of that bald man licking what must be, given her overwhelming presence in the book, the material girl's platform shoe, particularly unattractive. And it is not as if I'm not aroused by his particular "look." If Madonna were actually in search of a hot bald man, either a muscular and earringed Mr. Clean cartoon or that adorable skinhead in Bruce LaBruce's *No Skin Off My Ass* would have made a much more interesting sex partner. But many of the participants in *Sex* seem to have been chosen either for their cultural currency as certain kinds of stars (the proposition being: wouldn't it be fun to see Madonna fucking a number of trendy models, rappers, and Eurotrash royalty—NOT!); or chosen for their shock value, evoking in the photographs a kind of "Diane Arbus goes to the Mineshaft" ethos. If one were actually interested in perusing erotically stimulating images of S/M sex, one could find better representations of most of these acts in garden-variety porno videos (see, for example, the work of Christopher Rage), or in publications such as *On Our Backs, Drummer*, or even *Queer Intercourse*, a local Pittsburgh 'zine—and at a significantly lower price.

The problem, of course, with *Sex* is that, on some level, it is just not foul enough. For many readers, it is exceedingly banal, serving up mostly familiar, almost lethargic fantasies in an arty kind of softcore porn style, or else the de-eroticized, self-absorbed, and bourgeois gaze of Arbus and her present day heir, David Lynch. Arbus, Lynch and *Sex* all share the middle class voyeur's privilege of rejecting the material comfort and safety of their natal background. This work partakes of a kind of desperate, foot-stomping, temper tantrum, a "watch me mommy and daddy, I can look at really horrible stuff and think it's cool" aesthetic. This aesthetic claims to rebel against middle class privilege, but it is actually—in its distance from, and lack of response (erotic or otherwise) to the "underground" world it explores—a reinstantiation of that very privilege. Take the freak show and put it on your living room wall. Turn your trip to a sex club into a coffee table book. On some level, this aesthetic is not really about sex at all, but about the transformation of sex into an emblem of privilege. Corporeal pleasure, sexual or otherwise, is not even its goal. It in fact expresses the very revulsion towards sexuality it claims to contest. Look how icky sex is, it proclaims, and look how close I can get to it without retching. The dissipated, pathetic figure of the aging businessman fondling Madonna's breast, accompanied by a text which suggests that only the acquisition of money could motivate sleeping with "two hundred fifty pounds, five seven, bald, disgusting misogynist pigs"; the leather-clad man in a sling drinking what is apparently urine from a high heeled shoe, set within the deep recesses of the photograph, distanced from the spectator, framed by the wooden beams which entrap him, and the ugliness of the scene emphasized by the numerous barbed staples pinning the image, like a collector's insect, to a white, pristine background; the bald and jeweled figure licking the skin of his chained and pierced partner, their eeriness emphasized by the x-ray style of the negative printing, photographed like creatures from another planet in a fifties sci-fi film. All of these images, which might have been photographed in such a way as to highlight their sensuality, are instead presented as a series of portraits of sexual freaks.

Such an aesthetic ultimately partakes of the perverse only insofar as it might be wielded against the father. The joys of perversity for its own sake, the transformation of the body into a surface of previously unimagined pleasures, the willing of the body into a site for experimentation and play are not even issues here. In its refusal to leave behind a relationship of conflict with the father, *Sex* represents a whiny tribute to Oedipus and the family romance. It deploys an anti-oedipal, polymorphous perversity only insofar as such a deployment might ultimately reinscribe the authority of the father to say no. This reinscription of the authority of the father is in fact a recurrent theme in Madonna's work, present in such songs as "Papa Don't Preach" and "Oh, Father," as well as the sequences in *Truth or Dare* which deal with the singer's family.

And, while that much abused organ, the clitoris, is mentioned a number of times in *Sex*, it never actually makes an appearance. This fact will undoubtedly give rise to a certain reading of this book as "subversive" in its refusal to make the clitoris visible for the pleasure of men. Has the continued cultural invisibility of the clitoris produced "subversive" opportunities for female pleasure, or has it assisted in the continued privileging of male pleasure in representations of sexuality? While both these readings carry some weight, my vote at this particular historical moment is for the latter. Such a vote is obviously shaped by my own ethics, as well as those ideological forces which I am less capable of articulating. In either case, merely invoking its name serves the purposes of the book. This suggests—as Foucault might say, and contrary to my argument with my mother—that merely talking about sex does not necessarily free us from anything.

## II.

As part of his attempt to understand the psychological structures of fascism, Georges Bataille has argued that social existence can be divided into two realms, the homogeneous and the heterogeneous. The homogeneous realm of social existence is the "useful" realm, and its foundation is money. In contrastto the homogeneous, Bataille conceives the heterogeneous world as the world of both the elevated (religion, militaristic and nationalistic spectacle, displays of sovereign power) and the profane (madness, delirium, and so-called "perverse" sexuality)— worlds which disrupt productive homogeneous society from both "above" and "below." Homogeneous society works to exclude all forms of heterogeneity, but it simultaneously attempts to make use of "free floating" elevated heterogeneous forms in the service of a greater homogeneity: Christmas, the Olympic Games, and rock concerts might represent instances of "productive" society deploying elevated heterogeneous forms so as to increase homogeneity. Bataille's analysis tends to privilege profane heterogeneous forms for their disruptive potential—but he insists that the line between elevated and profane forms of heterogeneity is always unstable.

In other words, productive capitalist society can make a

limited and contained use of certain heterogeneous elements— elements such as the spectacle of S/M, gay and lesbian, and interracial sex—in the service of a greater homogeneity. Such a use requires that formerly discredited cultural forms be "elevated," through, among other means, specific practices of representation, to the status of a media event which might successfully be marketed to a mass audience. The figure of Madonna—the material girl, not the Virgin—represents, like Bataille's body of Christ, a cultural trope which seems capable in this historical moment of being mobilized in the service of either an elevated or profane heterogeneity. (Madonna's relationship to Christianity is obviously relevant here. Her objection to Sinead O'Connor's recent destruction of the Pope's photograph is evidence of her continued commitment to a contained deployment of Catholic symbol, ritual, and guilt.)

Madonna's work has in the past produced readings, reactions, and responses which testify to its anti-productivity, its transgression of certain cultural norms such as reproductive sexuality and stable gender identities. Yet the place of her work within homogeneous (capitalist) society, as well as its re-inscription of certain (hetero)sexual norms, makes possible a continued containment of its free-floating excess. The "failure" of Madonna's *Sex* is linked to the book's attempt to mass market a profane heterogeneity through a redundant deployment of the icon named Madonna. In other words, what renders *Sex* not perverse enough is its particular deployment of the figure of Madonna and its accompanying star persona. Such a deployment threatens to make the "impure" world of the perverse useful for a contained consumption by homogeneous capitalist culture.

I realize that my assumption of the text's "failure" rests on at least two other related assumptions: first, that the book's intention was in fact to create engaging and arousing representations of sexuality; and second, that I am in some sense a member of its "proper" audience, a reader who was at least initially positioned to read "with," rather than "against" the text. Concerning the first assumption, I would only want to say here that the perhaps cynical reading of *Sex*—that it is in fact not intended to arouse at all, but rather designed to evoke the impossibility of sex in an age haunted by the threat of HIV disease—is somewhat beside the point, a rather simplistic and flat reading of the text, and not one which suggests many interesting possibilities. Like most gay men, my life has been irrevocably altered by the disease; I really don't need a fifty dollar book to remind me that sex today is not what it used to be. Concerning the second assumption, I understand the "something for everyone" style of the book as an invitation suggesting that I am, on at least some level, an appropriate reader. The photographs make reference to a number of cultural practices with which I am familiar and in which I am positioned, practices associated with what we might schematically refer to as the urban gay male community. On the level of style, the book refers intertextually to a number of familiar sources, including pornography, coffee table art books, and *Interview* magazine.

The problem with *Sex* is not merely its attempt to mass market heterogeneity, for there are in fact mass-marketed cultural forms such as pornography which are "successful" in that they do what *Sex* doesn't. That is, they arouse. Nor is *Sex*'s problem the figure of Madonna herself, for some of the most "successful" photographs are those in which she appears alone, those which highlight her chameleon-like ability to transform herself into a multiplicity of images of women. These photographs include one of Madonna kneeling nude on the beach, coifed in gold hoop earrings and a Brigitte Bardot/Ursula Andress/Sharon Tate wig; another in which, naked, she stands astride a fish-shaped fountain; the one in which she stands atop a radiator, dressed in ankle boots and a white tee shirt; and the photograph in which she dangles from a hang glider of sorts.

I must confess that, of these four photographs, I find only the first two particularly compelling. But a significant number of other gay men have testified to the pleasure they got from these photographs. These photographs all show a Madonna who has, either through disguise or through the rendering of the body itself as kind of objet d'art, managed to escape the burden of the historical person Madonna, evoking, not coincidentally, some of the least familiar images of the singer. (Not sur-

prisingly, a number of my friends, both gay and straight, male
and female, who saw these particular photographs, wondered
aloud if in fact the image "really is" Madonna.)

But, in the majority of the book's photographs, the particular historical convergence of media-manic Madonna with the
realm of the perverse leads to *Sex*'s particular brand of eroticism, an eroticism which seems disturbingly familiar, bland,
and devoid of either passion or experimentation. Like Lucy
traveling to London to wear miniskirts and see the Dave Clark
Five, Madonna travels, in *Sex*, through a variety of sexual locales and styles of representation. Lucy's travels to London,
however, did not take as their object the pursuit of "perverse"
sexual fantasies. And Madonna is clearly not Lucy—she lacks
Ball's comic subtlety. Even when *Sex* attempts humor, there is
very little camp here, and instead, too much vulgarity posing as
camp. What makes camp interesting is its ability to solicit a variety of affective responses, including humor, seriousness,
irony, and even arousal, all in a form which deftly combines
spectacle and subtlety. (Some gay theorists have advanced the
position that camp is antithetical to arousal. I would counter
this reading by pointing to a number of cultural texts, including
Cher, gay porno films set in military schools and boot camps,
and even Madonna's own "Justify My Love" video.) But the
humor of *Sex* is largely the humor of the bathroom, in which
proper bourgeois sensibilities are both shocked and amused by
obvious and vulgar displays of transgression: Madonna straddling a dog, Madonna dressed as a Catholic school girl being as-
saulted by two crude skinheads, Madonna hitchhiking in the
nude, Madonna pumping gas with her tits exposed. In all these
photographs, Madonna performs for the camera as Madonna,
shocking only the sensibilities of those who are completely unfamiliar with explicit representations of sexuality and the body,
and amusing only those who are in a position to laugh at such
unfamiliarity. Like my high school friend Monique, who often
yelled "lick my clit" at passing strangers out the window of my
car, Madonna is, in *Sex*, a one-joke comedienne. Each of these
situations contains the potential for a camp treatment, but
Madonna frustrates each one, interrupting each illusion by

drawing too much attention to herself and her ever-inflating ego.

It is, after all, Madonna's version of sex which this book takes as its subject: Madonna the star visits sex the foreign land. What the photographs in the book most resemble are your second cousin's recent vacation slides. Like all such images, they are chiefly of interest only to the sentimental traveler; for the rest of us they are rather boring. After a while, the various tunnels and towers all start to resemble one another. We sit through the photographs politely, trying to find a point of entry or interest, but the best we can manage is to stifle our yawn and flip through them as rapidly as possible.

## III.

Madonna's work undoubtedly represents a boon to recent cultural criticism because it seems to embody, and be embroiled in, numerous contradictions. University-based criticism in particular is these days focused on "contradiction": rejecting the tradition, associated with the Frankfurt School, of finding in the texts of mass culture only the most disturbing and debilitating cultural and political tendencies, criticism in the seventies began exploring both the ways in which such texts might actually resist dominant ideologies, as well as the complicated operations required to read the texts of mass culture. A number of positions associated with poststructuralism—Foucault's reformulation of power as "productive," Antonio Gramsci's and Louis Althusser's reformulations of questions of political struggle, deconstruction's insistence that the itinerary of reading one brings to a text necessarily shapes one's posited explanation—all of these have reinforced the sense that popular culture is neither "reactionary" nor "progressive," but the site of contradictory ideologies.

When I first saw *Sex*, I anticipated a number of contradictory critical responses. The "against pornography" crowd, consisting of such strange bedfellows as members of the religious right, and feminists of a variety of genders and sexual orientations, such as Gloria Steinem, Andrea Dworkin, John Stoltenberg, and Susan Griffin, would find the book offensive. Liberal criticism which champions most any and all representations of sexuality (excluding those involving children, animals, and the dead) would call the book liberatory. Another critical response might celebrate the polymorphous perversity Madonna explores in the text; still another might critique her blatant appropriation of culturally marginalized sexualities for monetary gain. From the more formally minded comes the argument that *Sex*'s strangely distracting style of representation (the multiplied images, the layering of text on top of photograph, the "unnatural" colors of some of the images, even the faulty binding) resists the (politically incorrect) desire of the spectator to gaze at and "objectify" bodies. Or, we might hear that *Sex* refuses to move beyond certain "artsy," fashionable, bourgeois norms of representation.

Even on the level of the individual photographs, *Sex* seems to invite wildly competing interpretations. Here are some of the readings I imagine might be generated by the photograph of Big Daddy Kane, Madonna, and Naomi Campbell, in which Kane, clad in a pair of paisley bikini briefs, appears to masturbate a nude Madonna, who is simultaneously French kissing an also nude Naomi Campbell, who has simultaneously placed her hand over Madonna's left breast:

1) The photograph is progressive in that it portrays interracial, non-monogamous, non-procreative bisexual sex.
2) The photograph is reactionary in that it portrays "lesbian" sex for the gaze and pleasure of a man. (Kane gazes at the two women while he fingers Madonna. The women gaze at one another.)
3) The photograph is progressive in that it portrays interracial lesbian sex, a largely unrepresented sexual practice.
4) The photograph is reactionary in that it portrays interracial lesbian sex, and thus extends the disciplinary gaze of modern society to new bodies.
5) The photograph is progressive in that it "deconstructs" the racist logic which casts black men as sexual predators by giving an image to this ideology. (In other words, the photograph as a culturally shaped representation strips bare an ideology which often remains hidden, naturalized, and

thus, through a de-naturalization, forces the spectator to confront that ideology.)

6) The photograph is reactionary in that it re-articulates the stereotype of the black man as sexual predator.

7) The photograph is progressive in that it refuses to reveal Kane's penis, and thus refuses to "reduce" the figure of the black man to his penis.

8) The photograph is reactionary in that it refuses to reveal Kane's penis, and thus maintains the lie of the equation "penis = phallus." (The logic which denies the fact that the organ "penis" cannot possibly live up to the mystique of the phallus.)

9) The photograph is reactionary in that it refuses to reveal Kane's penis, and thus denies a certain genital sexuality to the figure of the black male.

10) The photograph is reactionary in that it refuses to reveal Kane's penis, and thus extends to the black male the privilege granted by mainstream culture to white men—the privilege to control the sexual scene from afar, and to act as a voyeur.

All the readings of the photograph as progressive might be tempered by Foucault's insistence that transgression is always necessarily both a re-inscription and testing of a limit. Transgression thus moves in a spiral. It does not move beyond the limit in any simple way, nor does it simply re-inscribe the limit as limit. But the problem with this strategy of reading for contradictions is that such readings often do not sufficiently consider their own conditions of possibility. The fact that a text is available for a variety of contradictory interpretations tells us little about to whom such readings are available, by what rules they are formulated, how one gains access to such rules, how the text might work formally or generically to contain its contradictions, and whether or not anyone is particularly "disturbed" by the contradictions to think or act differently.

In trying to think about this picture's power to disturb, it's important to note its resemblance to softcore heterosexual pornography, characterized by its avoidance of the male genitals, its deployment of clothed men and naked women (most of the naked male bodies in the book appear in the photographs of the Gaiety theater gay boys), and its "lesbian" scenes staged for the benefit of a male spectator (in this case, a male spectator "in" the text). This, I would argue, is in fact the predominant aesthetic of the whole of *Sex* and *not just* of this particular photograph. What is perhaps interesting is the presence of such a photograph in a book which has proclaimed itself to be so transgressive, so radical, so daring. Thus, while I would avoid labeling the photograph itself as either "transgressive" or "reactionary," I would still submit that its portrayal of sexuality is familiar, not particularly arousing, and not all that interesting. Certainly not worth fifty dollars, to say the least.

Barry Walters's recent insistence in *The Advocate* that Madonna represents "pop's most vocal exponent of AIDS awareness and general queerocity"—this particular reading of the diva representing that now-familiar attempt to create Madonna as some kind of transgressive figure—is surely a comment on the paucity of queer erotic representations in pop music. My first response to *Sex* was, frankly, one of shame and embarrassment. Here were a variety of "perverse" sexual representations which apparently did nothing for me. What was wrong with me? Why could I not respond "appropriately" to these images? Perhaps I was just too gay for Madonna. I wondered if I'd erotically fallen victim to a certain reactionary tendency in gay liberation which characterizes gay sexuality as utterly separate and distinct by nature from straight sexuality. Perhaps I had lost my ability to respond to representations of the opposite sex. Perhaps I was a victim of the binary logic of sexuality!

Of course I knew better. Recently I spent a good deal of time reading erotica written for women by women, erotica which featured no images of gay male sexuality whatsoever, and yet which I found to be extremely pleasurable, indeed arousing. Admittedly, this erotica was not of the stroker variety usually featured in skin magazines, gay and straight. There was a great deal more care taken with the language than is usual in such stories, more I suppose of what people call plot, character, and description. There was simultaneously, however, a great deal of explicit sexual description in these stories. Images from the stories returned to me a number of times that summer, often, while I was making love with my partner, images which would suggest new activities and sensations, new positions, new roles, a certain atmosphere of sensuality that would animate our lovemaking. While the stories did not compel me to have sex with women, they did encourage me in my efforts with my lover. If I had in fact lost my capacity to respond erotically to images of women, how could I explain the pleasure with which I read and reread these stories?

And of course I should note that the photographs of the gay men in *Sex* are themselves not particularly arousing or interesting. While the men at the Gaiety are admittedly hot, at least as far as conventional porn stars go, they are photographed in such a way as to blunt their eroticism. For example, only a single flaccid penis appears in the pages of *Sex*, and only a handful of asses, few of them photographed so as to accentuate their shape, muscularity, or voluptuousness. (One of the most beautiful asses in the book is interrupted by a clowning Madonna, who just can't resist mugging for the camera.) The bodies of most of the men are crowded out by the presence of Madonna, whose breasts, ass, legs and vulva figure prominently throughout the book. When photographs of naked men embracing do appear, they are multiplied with the banality of Warhol's dollar bills and/or interrupted by the voice of Madonna emphasizing not their eroticism, but their political correctness, and assuring the reader as to their prowess as, of all things, dancers.

I am not suggesting here that there is a single effective way to represent sexuality, or that representations of sexuality are not themselves embedded in cultural ideologies that we might want to interrogate and explore. In other words, I recognize that I tend to respond positively to what are fairly standard means of representing the nude male body—Herb Ritts, Bruce Weber, etc.—and that the limits of such representations, and the conflicting ideologies they embody, need to be elaborated. But it is difficult to attribute the "failure" of the representations in *Sex* to the fact that they challenge conventional means of representing sexuality. In fact, they seem primarily to represent watered

down versions of all-too-familiar representational strategies—
as I have already suggested, straight, softcore pornography of
the Playboy Channel variety, in which the nude male body is
avoided at every possible moment, and in which only an occa-
sional flaccid penis manages to interrupt the male spectator's
continued contemplation of the female body. And I find it particularly telling that my initial response to the book was one of
shame, not at being "caught looking," but at failing somehow to
be "adequate" to this defensively heterotextual text.

## IV.

Astride the stairmaster at the YMCA (reported to be one of
Madonna's favorite forms of exercise), I read with interest *Vanity Fair*'s preview to *Sex*. Seeing those tongue-in-cheek parodies
of fifties *Playboy* layouts, I imagined *Sex* would be a kind of
playful tribute to the work of Cindy Sherman. Like Sherman's
work, these photographs emphasized the imaging of women and
drew attention to historically specific styles of representation.
In other words, they did not attempt to pass themselves off as
"realistic" images of women, but instead highlighted, through
their deployment of a style which marks itself as belonging to
the past, the fact that erotic representations of women are
structured by prevailing styles and conventions, conventions
which, while they are perhaps erotically pleasing, must also be
interrogated for what they might suggest about the multiple
and contradictory roles of women as cultural image. The eroticism of the photographs came from their sense of play, their
willingness to inhabit—but not merely inhabit—a set of cultural ideas about sexuality. These photographs expressed a
camp sensibility, a kind of distance from the image which, in its
emphasis on the photograph as constructed image rather than
simple record of the real, suggested perhaps that sexuality represents not a natural, biological and/or inevitable series of be-
haviors and responses, but a learned set, a set which, while imposed on the sexual subject, is open to an admittedly
circumscribed and restricted experimentation, re-negotiation,
and transformation.

Unfortunately, very few of the images in *Sex* have any of the playfulness of the *Vanity Fair* photos. A number of them come close. The Brigitte Bardot wig certainly helps, as do the gray flannel suits. This kind of drag emphasizes the image as image, and the possibilities for experimentation within the sexual patterns and roles proposed by and imposed on the sexual subject. But in general the photographs in *Sex* lack the spectacle-value of camp because Madonna the loud-mouthed, self-promoting child, embarrassingly eager for attention, keeps interrupting the pleasure of the spectacle, disrupting the game by re-establishing the very ego which the sexual, in its messy confusion of boundaries, threatens to undo. In most of the photographs, there is just too much of a certain Madonna.

Concerning the written text accompanying the photographs, I can't help wondering: has anyone actually managed to read all of this book? Not only is the written text painfully juvenile, interspersing the most predictable kinds of "pornographic" declarations—such as "I'm feeling very relaxed cause Ingrid just ate my pussy"—with philosophical ruminations like "But he gave me crabs. That's what you get. So you win some and you lose some," or "But I have friends who have money and are educated and they stay in abusive relationships, so they must be getting something out of it." The text often works against itself, making the stories at times almost painfully difficult to decipher. (This fact will undoubtedly produce an interpretation of *Sex* as "really" about resisting our nasty "masculinist" urges to play voyeur.) The more pomo than homo visual style of *Interview* magazine, the excessive stylistic play, is frankly non-erotic. The layering of text over image, and the varying styles, shapes, colors, and sizes in the typeface of the prose, as well as the multiply exposed, colored, doubled photographs—all seem to serve no purpose other than to ape *Interview*'s too-hip-for-real-life style. Like the hyped up techno style of nineties club kids, or indeed like Madonna's own *Erotica* album, the style of *Sex* is cerebral, mechanistic, trendy, perhaps even ugly, designed to distract the reader enough so that she or he will forget how really boring the book and its accompanying version of sex really is. Not to mention the fact that the stock on which the book is printed is extremely cheap, and not particularly pleasurable to the touch. I know a number of queens who, feeling completely ripped off by the broken promises of *Sex*, would like to read Madonna.

## V.

In his study of the writings of the Marquis de Sade and Leopold von Sacher-Masoch, Gilles Deleuze attempts to differentiate between sadism and masochism as both "perversions" and aesthetic forms. According to Deleuze, sadomasochism is a misnomer, a mistaken attempt to conflate what are in fact two distinctly different imaginings of the relationship between sexuality and cruelty. According to Deleuze, the fact that violence is present in both sadism and masochism should not lead us to conclude, as others have done, that the two perversions unite to form one. As Deleuze suggests, "no doctor would treat a fever as though it were a definite symptom of a specific disease; he views it rather as though it were an indeterminate syndrome common to a number of possible diseases." Thus, the qualitative differences between sadism and masochism must be examined.

One way we might pursue this goal is to explore the very different aesthetic structures which these two perversions employ. Each "disease" was named after a specific writer, each of whose works, according to Deleuze, embody distinctively different styles. As Deleuze has suggested, "The genius of Sade and Masoch are poles apart; their worlds do not communicate, and as novelists their techniques are totally different." Just as it makes no sense to speak of sadomasochism as a single perversion, similarly it would be misguided to describe a text such as *Sex* as "sadomasochistic." Instead, we should argue that the text, in its combining of sexuality and violence, deploys *either* a sadistic or masochistic aesthetic, *or* some as yet unnamed aesthetic which works through yet another relationship between sexuality and cruelty.

Deleuze notes, among other things, the repetitiveness in Sade's style of writing, the monotony of sadism, and the apathy of the sadist. He links these characteristics of the sadist to the fact that the sadistic libertine's goal is not to convince, persuade, or educate, but to instruct. Sadistic writing is

characterized by a demonstrative use of language, bearing
witness to the desire of the sadist to show "that reasoning is itself a form of violence, and that he [sic] is on the side of violence, however calm and logical he may be. He is not even attempting to prove anything to anyone, but to perform a
demonstration related essentially to the solitude and omnipotence of its author.... Whether he is among his accomplices or
among his victims, each libertine, while engaged in reasoning,
is caught in the hermetic circle of his own solitude and unique-
ness...." As Bataille said of Sade and sadistic language, "It is a
language which repudiates any relationship between speaker
and audience."

The sadist is thus characterized by a self-absorbed distance from the sexual scene and its victims, and by an interest
in a pure and disinterested demonstration of reason through violence and sexuality. Sadism attempts to deploy a combination
of sexuality and violence in the service of a cold and demonstrative reason. It might be argued, in fact, that the goal of
sadism is not sexual pleasure at all, not even the sadist's sexual
pleasure, but a negation of everything—even the sexual—an
"ideal" negation which, owing to the limits of negation in nature, can only be achieved, ideally, through reason. (According
to Deleuze, the sadist realizes that, in nature, there is no such
thing as pure negation: "Destruction is merely the reverse of
creation and change, disorder is another form of order, and the
decomposition of death is equally the composition of life.") This
pursuit of the idea of negation leads the sadist to accelerate violence and multiply victims and their sufferings. But the sadist
realizes that such a multiplication can never achieve, in the
real, the idea of pure negation: "Hence the rage and despair of
the sadistic hero when he realizes how paltry his own crimes
are in relation to the idea which he can only reach through the
omnipotence of reasoning."

Perhaps the redundancy of much of *Sex*—the miniature,
multiplied, repetitive, and ultimately banal photographs of
Madonna engaging in bondage scenes with two dyke skinheads,
Madonna lying in bed between two naked, lithe and androgy-
nous men, Madonna admiring the muscles of a shackled man in

a leather vest, Madonna surrounded by a bevy of both naked and tuxedoed gay boy-toy admirers at the Gaiety theater, Madonna cavorting with two beautiful gray flannel "lesbians" at the seashore, etc., etc., etc., as well as the flat, repetitive, artless and demonstrative quality of much of *Sex*'s prose—perhaps all of this might be attributable to the text's portrayal of Madonna as the sadistic heroine. Again, according to Deleuze's argument, it is not the *presence* of violence per se that might lead one to read Madonna as the sadistic heroine here, for masochism too is marked by violence. It is rather the *quality* of the depicted violence which is significant here. While Madonna is present in nearly every photograph, she seems to function not so much as a participant, but as an instructor. She stands back from the depicted scenes, enclosed in the hermetic circle of her own star persona, reveling not in the pleasure the sexual scene might contain, but in the demonstration of her own freedom and privilege to enter these forbidden enclaves, and in a certain enjoyment of her own role as instructor there.

There are a number of ways in which the photographs emphasize Madonna's separation from the sexual activity taking place around her, and stress her role as instructor—even when she is "playing" victim. Her blond hair, pale skin, glamour girl make-up and see-through body suit contrast starkly with the two dark, topless, black jeans-clad lesbians, with their pierced nipples and ears, shaved heads, and tattoos. (Is it merely a coincidence that, in a book which features a number of "lesbian" scenarios, Madonna is never photographed with a woman who resembles her even superficially? Not a single other blond woman appears in *Sex*.) In most of the photographs in which the three women appear together, Madonna is at the center of the frame, a kind of self-absorbed spectacle distanced from the sexual activity occurring around her. At the Gaiety Theater, she is the lone female privileged enough to trespass. She enjoys "gay male strip places"; she admires from a distance the slim and beautiful bodies of the skilled dancers. There is no mention here of any sexual pleasure she might get from these bodies, nor is it ever suggested in any of the photographs that any kind of sexual activity might occur here in which she might participate. As with the photographs of the two butch dykes, Madonna is at the center of almost every image, orchestrating the action with her riding crop, extending her gloved hands to the men gathered around her, and occasionally they, perhaps against the orders of their instructor, seem distracted by one another's (or their own) beauty. The sole clothed female among a group of largely naked, largely dark men, Madonna with her blond ambition interrupts the clandestine (homo)sexual activities usually occurring at the strip theater with a display of the star's own power to control and manipulate the scene. Clearly, she's not here to get off—at least not sexually. In many of the photographs in which she appears with others, Madonna is placed at the foreground of the image, emphasizing her role as instructor as well as her distance from the scene. While Madonna, in the foreground and dressed in a teddy, looks out of the frame in the direction of the spectator, the two pierced dykes, naked, look at her. In the majority of the photographs featuring Naomi Campbell and Big Daddy Kane, a front and center pale-skinned Madonna is framed by the two blacks, her blond radiance set off by their dark skin. In the "Dita in the Chelsea Girl" comic book section of the text, Madonna almost always occupies the foreground of the sexual play, occasionally turning directly to the camera to record her reactions to the scene.

In Deleuze's analysis of sadism, the female sadist acts as the representative of the father. According to Deleuze, "the paternal and patriarchal theme undoubtedly predominates in sadism." Deleuze approvingly cites Pierre Klossowski's insistence that "the sadistic phantasy ultimately rests on the theme of the father destroying his own family, by inciting the daughter to torture and murder the mother," and argues that what makes Sade's heroines sadistic is their "sodomitic union with the father in a fundamental alliance against the mother." Without resorting to a specious armchair form of psychoanalysis, we might again notice the relationship of conflict and ambivalence between the cultural image called Madonna and her father, the repeated attempts by the daughter to win the father over, the desperate attempts by the daughter to secure the father's attention and love.

Unlike the masochistic scenario, in which we are dealing "with a victim in search of a torturer," a victim who "needs to educate, persuade and conclude an alliance with the torturer in order to realize the strangest of schemes," we are often faced, in *Sex*, with the figure of the sadistic libertine, the apathetic, distanced, figure condemned to "accelerate and condense" her sexual activities in an effort to negate even the sexual. Perhaps what *Sex* needs is more of what Deleuze characterizes as masochism, with its emphasis on suspense, ritual, and spectacle. Deleuze suggests that "the art of suspense always places us on the side of the victim and forces us to identify with him, whereas the gathering momentum of repetition tends to force us on to the side of the torturer and make us identify with the sadistic hero." Perhaps what renders *Sex* so dissatisfying is its placement of the spectator on the side of the sadist. For those who find, in sex, the pleasure of a gratification delayed almost to the point of pain, who proceed, by contractual agreement, to educate and persuade their sexual partners to become the cold and authoritarian figure they adore, *Sex*, in its emphasis on repetition, demonstration, and self-absorption, is simply not erotic.

## VI.

Three years ago, I was invited to read my fiction at Hemingway's, a Pittsburgh bar and restaurant named after the macho hero of American letters. Not knowing what to read at this ostensibly straight establishment, I consulted with one of my closest friends, a lesbian. She suggested that I read a particular passage from my second novel (the one my mother has sometimes described as trashy) that recounts two men making love. My friend paid me the extreme and perhaps inflated compliment that this passage represented for her one of the most sensuous accounts of two men fucking that she had ever read. While I distrusted her overly enthusiastic evaluation of my work—she was, after all, a close friend and one who was perhaps not likely to have read many fictional accounts of two men fucking—I trusted her polymorphous perversity enough to follow her advice, and read the following passage. (The novel, *When the Parrot Boy Sings*, is set in the early eighties, when we had only a dim awareness of the impending dangers of HIV disease and how to prevent the spread of the HIV virus.)

That same morning, I called Dennis from a pay phone, and took the subway to his apartment. As usual, he answered the door in his underwear.

"Busy night?" he asked.

"Shut up," I said as I kissed his cheek and grabbed him between the legs. I led him by his dick, down the hall, and into the bedroom.

I fell on top of him, kissing him as I pulled off my pants and pushed my hips into his. He took my balls in his hands and pulled the skin between his fingers. As I lifted my shirt up over my head, he bit my nipples roughly. I responded by taking his head in my hands, and pushing it tighter against me.

"Let me fuck you," he said as he reached in the nightstand drawer for a tube of KY.

"No. I'm afraid."

"I won't hurt you." He ran his hands over my ass, pressing his fingers inside me.

"I don't know. What if something happens?"

"I won't come inside you. Come on, don't be afraid." He smeared the lube over his cock, and then into me. I hesitated. There was something so arousing about his pleading, and the fact that he didn't seem to care that I wasn't sure if I wanted him inside me. He pulled me up onto my knees, and entered me slowly from behind.

I lowered my arms to the bed, resting on my elbows, and pushing my weight as hard as I could back into him. I could feel the sweat dripping down my legs as he moved in and out of me. It was almost like a struggle, this testing of our separate strengths against each other, he pushing forward as I pushed back.

"Let me get on top of you," I said.

Pinning him beneath me, I forced him deeper inside my body, and quickened the rhythm of our movement. The springs of the mattress were making so much noise I thought the neighbors would hear us.

"I can't hold back with you on top of me like that," he said as he pulled my cock.

Suddenly, I didn't care anymore if just this once he came inside me. I wanted to be the one to decide when he would reach his orgasm, I wanted to see him, to watch his face as he lost himself in me. I pushed myself even harder and faster down on him, and as I heard his breathing quicken and felt his movements become even more intense, I let myself come in the air, so that the muscles inside me would tighten around his dick. And just as I felt those muscles constrict, he stopped his moving and thrust himself just one more time inside me, holding his cock perfectly still as he came, his heart beating so strongly I could see it moving in his chest, and the palms of his hands and the nape of his neck flushed crimson with a rash.

During the course of my reading, two people walked out. They had been in the middle of the crowd, and so their exit was duly noted by the rest of the audience. I was mortified. I felt ashamed, as if I had transgressed the appropriate boundaries of public behavior by bringing out into the open activities which had best remain "private," as if I had revealed inappropriate details about my personal life, and as if I had made my writing itself vulnerable to the criticism that it is both "confessional" (and thus, trivial) and not well crafted. Even today, I find this an extremely difficult passage to read; it resembles all too closely what I fear is a perhaps "artless" gay pornography. I try to silence doubts by reminding myself that this was in fact one of my intentions in writing the novel, which attempts to combine competing generic approaches such as pornography, satire, social commentary, and melodrama. While this is true—I was in fact reading Bakhtin's work on Menippean satire at the time I was writing this novel—this account still has the ring (to my ears, at least) of what psychobabble sometimes casts as "rationalizing."

I have recently sent copies of this novel to several schools in the hope of securing a job as a teacher of fiction writing. As I remember this, I think, "Oh my God, what was I thinking? Who in their right mind is going to offer me a job after seeing this pornography?" This response arises in part from the fact that most of the writing I have done "outside" of the academy has an extremely contradictory relationship to my work within the university. My prose fiction in particular has rarely been acknowledged there. Its status as "gay writing," and a gay writing which is largely untutored or at least self-taught, has led me sometimes to make apologies for my work, as well as to feel "illegitimate," marginalized, a phony who can fool the market, but not those true arbiters of taste who frequently inhabit university M.F.A. programs in Creative Writing in particular.

To read my conflicting responses to my own work and its place within and outside of the university as "internalized homophobia" is perhaps to cast the problem as one of personal responsibility and pathology, and, in so doing, to dull the very real ways in which my feelings are in some sense required and produced by the current competing and contradictory cultural understandings of homosexuality. Considering the current climate, it is only fitting that I should be embarrassed by my work. It is appropriate, given the attempts of a liberal culture to manage sexual difference by relegating it to the status of the private, that I should feel *as if* I had behaved inappropriately by reading aloud an account of two men fucking. It is fitting, given the attempts by the university to "manage" diversity by creating "special" fields of knowledge such as gay studies, that I should feel *as if* my work is marginal to the more serious and legitimate interests of the academy. The important thing is not that I necessarily reconcile, through recourse to a humanist psychotherapy, my feelings with my behavior, but that I continue to behave, despite my feelings, *as if* my work in fiction is not marginal, but central; *as if* my "gay" writing is not pornographic and illegitimate, but important and worthy of valorization; *as if* discussions of sexuality in general, and gay sexuality in particular, belong not to the private, but to the public realm. Such an impossible attempt to wrestle homosexuality to the center of discussions of sexuality works not to create a new center, nor to include homosexuality in some ever-expanding universalist conception of the human, but to jam the theoretical machine that produces margin and center in the first place, and to move us towards that impossible attempt to think through questions of difference outside of hierarchy.

Following my reading at Hemingway's, a fellow gay writer complimented me on the fact that my writing had driven two people to leave. He argued that this was proof that my work had significantly moved these two people, even if it was the case that it had moved them right out the door. While I am extremely suspicious of the facility with which gay culture sometimes privileges its own often highly commodified cultural productions as "oppositional," I am not quite prepared to say that reading accounts of gay men fucking, in a place called Hemingway's where such things are rarely spoken of, is necessarily an inappropriate or ineffective gesture. While I would not want to call the gesture "political" (especially given the ways in which that term increasingly refers, in certain academic circles, to everything *but* collective action), I am still interested in attempting to think through the relationship between such "individual" gestures and the struggle for political transformation, the multiple and conflicting cultural meanings attached to the homosexual, and the ways in which this category, impossibly purged of its essentialist trappings, might produce in particular contexts effects which we might hesitatingly cast as "oppositional."

Relatively late in the film *Body of Evidence*, when asked why she ultimately broke off her affair with an older, wealthy gentleman, the character played by Madonna bursts into tears as she confesses that she caught her former lover in bed with another man. Despite the fact that she and this man engaged in a variety of sexual activities which included scenes of bondage and domination, the sexually adventurous defendant accused of fucking a man to death exclaims that she could not possibly cope with the thought of her lover in bed with another man. All through her trial, the character's sexual activities have been narrated at some length to the jury, as well as portrayed for the enjoyment of the film's audience through her burgeoning relationship with the character of her lawyer, played by Willem Dafoe. Those activities include "straight" sex, adultery and public sex, and involve the use of sexually explicit videos, belts, hot wax, handcuffs, and broken glass. It is this pivotal moment on the witness stand, however, in which the poor wronged woman expresses her horror at having caught her lover in bed with anther man, and laments her inability to compete with such a man, which momentarily secures for this sometimes unlikable character the sympathy of the judge, jury, and perhaps even the implied audience of the film. Sex between men is just too much for Madonna.

Similarly, in her final letter to her lover John, Dita, one of Madonna's alter-egos, and, presumably, the one who structures most of *Sex*, writes of her horror at having secretly witnessed him being blown by another man. While she confesses at first that "I didn't know if I was turned on or disgusted," she concludes her letter with "I think I'm gonna be sick. Next time you want pussy, just look in the mirror." This seems uncharacteristically prudish and narrow-minded for Dita, who, throughout *Sex*, has celebrated her own polymorphous perversity in a series of letters recounting for Johnny her lovemaking with her friend Ingrid. Dita in fact claims throughout the book to be a real authority on sex. She tells us early on in the text that she is a "love technician" who will teach us how to fuck, and, in a conversation with a doctor, claims to be an authority on ass fucking in particular. In a text supposedly devoted to the pleasures of sex, the hip, and the shocking, an expression of revulsion at the image of two men caught in a sexual act (*sans* Madonna/Dita, no less), as well as the use of one of the most blatantly misogynist and heterosexist forms of insult ("pussy"), is interesting again perhaps chiefly *because* it appears in a book which claims to be so hip, so shocking, so sexy. As a gay man, I have to admit I took a certain pleasure in this particular portrayal of homosexuality—one suggesting the continued difficulty of recuperating the impure and filthy heterogeneity of male homosexuality for an elevated, capitalist consumption. That is, if even the hip Dita/Madonna thinks it's gross to be a gay man, perhaps there is still something worthwhile to be said for it.

## CAROL A. QUEEN

# Talking About *Sex*

I wonder if any other readers of Madonna's *Sex* stopped reading to masturbate.

If I'm the only one who did, no wonder so many reviews seem to miss the point. *Sex* has been both excoriated as pornography and ridiculed for not being erotic enough. But few of the reviewers and pundits who took on the large task of steering the public through the experience of *Sex* are accustomed to writing thoughtful analyses of pornography. Or erotica. Or whatever this almost-explicit, heavy handful of dreams ought to be called.

If anyone *had* found *Sex* appealing enough to set the book aside, turn the bell down on the phone, switch on the Magic Wand for a fast buzz or unzip the trousers for a quick wank, would it be widely considered appropriate in a book review or opinion piece to say so? Would this be considered a plus?

I have been considering these questions ever since I switched off the vibrator this afternoon. Sex and art make powerful, evocative bedfellows, but they don't usually make for very cogent art criticism, largely because sex has a language and logic with which many are unfamiliar, to which many are hostile, of which many are afraid. I fear these impairments have many commentators hogtied as surely as Allistair and Julie (the book's ballyhooed "lesbian skinheads") have Madonna trussed to her chair. But even those reviewers who responded to the eroticism of Madonna's collaboration with Meisel, Baron, and her cast of revelers don't tell me what I want to know: at what point did *you* put the book aside? What got you hard? What made you wet? Where did you insert yourself into the action, or what did you watch with the greatest emotion? What page had you flipped to when your palms got sweaty enough to slip on the book's metal covers, and how hot did they get under your hands?

For me it was the beach scene, that effortless lesbian seduction while the sun beat down. I had to go do myself because, unexpectedly, "The sky is the color of pussy." I had to do myself because she parted the strange girl's legs, vulva and ass cheeks, and because I wondered if anyone could see them, and because it crossed my mind to picture myself in each of their places in turn. And because she was drunk, I wondered if she'd be flushed with shame when she sobered up. And because I wondered if she and the stranger would go back to the hotel, feed each other scampi in the dining room, scandalize the rich old tourists, and spend the night together fucking.

Of course, I had already paged through half the book. Doubtless each image had worked its own subliminal erotic spell on me. *Sex* is a wonderful advertisement for masturbation—in fact, it's practically a primer. If you didn't get enough of Madonna with her hand in her pants during the Blond Ambition tour, you'll note with satisfaction that she celebrates the solitary pleasure throughout *Sex*. Her relationship with her pussy merits outspoken devotion and inspires a soliloquy about her youthful discovery of autoeroticism: "Honey poured from my 14-year-old gash and I wept," she writes, marrying pornography and poetry—two genres that were very important to me when I was the one weeping, touching, tasting. Here was the gift of a long-unfondled memory; I had to put the book down that time just to sit and remember what it was like to be fourteen and crazy with the profoundest new pleasure of my life.

The "young Madonna" photos that follow, especially the picture where she's captured spread over a mirror, show a much different side to her self-pleasuring than we get to see on stage or in *Truth or Dare*, where she's a grown-up piston high on exhibitionism. Don't other reviewers remember the time when they first dared to prop a mirror up to watch themselves do it? Pity if they've forgotten (and, I must say, if they've never tried).

Even rolling around on a Miami lawn, humping her platform shoe, Madonna is a winning ambassador for masturbation. It's hardly surprising that I felt such permission from the book. It moves me when someone tries to speak to sex, which is so overworked and at the same time so ignored, so skirted; it moves me more when the sex spoken to is not what I'm able to see every day. Even when the attempt falls short, my conversations with sex are bolstered by knowing that others try. I take it for granted that the interchange will be complex and often difficult for nearly everyone. Even Madonna. The ones for whom it seems simple are the ones, I think, who try not to engage very deeply in it.

Scanning the array of print responses to *Sex* which began appearing shortly before the book's publication, I find precious few people who seem to view sex the way I do, and many whose vantage points seem worlds away from the Madonna team's. Virtually all of them are prepared to make a loud declaration about what's erotic about the book (not much) and what's objectionable. It seems that if they find nothing to hail as erotic in *Sex*, the shrillness level of the criticism rises—as if they hoped and expected *their* secret hearts to be captured in Meisel's lens. They make no secret of their disappointment, but they're blaming it on Madonna, as if there was only *one* sexuality (instead of myriad), one definition of eroticism, and she's represented it all wrong.

So many people desperately want an erotica that speaks to them. Many others want, just as fiercely, *not* to be moved by erotica at all. When they get hold of *Sex* and find that it misses the mark of their yearnings—*or* that it hones in too close—their bitterness spills into the already cloudy water of that strange draught called "cultural criticism." I have drunk so much of this stuff in recent days that I'm afraid I'm feeling a little bitter, too—but not about the spendy Mylar candy bar. About the furor.

I want to reduce everything—at first—to "what you jacked off to" for a reason. I want to know what the critics had hoped to see. Each of us, I hope, has a pornographic imagination (if we have none, why the hell are we reviewing this book?), a stockpile (or at least a small heap) of scenes and images that we mentally riffle through when passion takes us. Each of us knows something we find erotic, even if it's so innocent or romantic that my calling it "pornographic" threatens to sully it. Madonna's private photo album may or may not closely resemble the one she's put into our hands—and our mental albums may or may not resemble hers. Unwittingly, but not surprisingly, most of the critics of *Sex* have told me more about their own eroticism than about Madonna's. I just wish they had spelled it out, not done it by default.

Why? Because trashing other people's sexual vision is so fucking common. It's the high-brows' lowest road. It's the little bit of fascism almost everyone is willing to embrace. We do it to each other, routinely, lightly, viciously, in and out of print. Too many of us do it to ourselves.

I don't know whether my sexuality very closely resembles Madonna's; Madonna-followers routinely project all kinds of things onto her, and I'm quite sure I'm no exception. I *do* know how strongly I responded to *Sex*. I know how wonderful it feels finally to see a book that I could purchase at a shopping mall speak directly to my lived and my fantasy sexuality. Fetishistic, responsive to powerplay, genderbent, onanistic and exhibitionistic, transcending oppositional categories of gay and straight, the book picks the brains of those whose complexly lived (or dreamed) eroticism has few, if any, mainstream artistic representatives. Or maybe Madonna is, quite simply, one of us.

My friend and colleague Lily Braindrop Burana, who publishes the omnisexual, fetish-friendly 'zine *Taste of Latex* ("all sexual flavors with no bitter aftertaste of apology"), was prepared to find in *Sex* a watered-down, hyped-up packaging of the sexual scene she documents so rawly and committedly. She worried that the book, like Madonna's video "Justify My Love," "would just look like our home movies on a good weekend." And it does! Neither of us realized until we saw the book how it would feel to see our sex reflected in the lens of mainstream culture. Is this why lesbians are thronging to their TVs to watch "Roseanne"? Women like us—bisexual dykes with a letch for gayboys, leatherwomen, exhibitionists, whose sexuality cooked for years in the crucible of gay men's porn but who search in vain for our reflections in the gay bookstore—are not even supposed to exist.

To the sexually adventurous female, the message sent by critics of *Sex* seems sticky with prurience and judgment. Madonna is called an exhibitionist as if that were a problem and not an inspiration, a pathology rather than a source of pleasure. I'm not prepared to judge whether there's a dysfunctional streak to Madonna's stardom (and frankly, I think it's pretty unseemly for folks whose status as cultural critics depends upon others' stardom to diss them for the qualities that put them there). I *am* prepared to evaluate the exhibitionism of *Sex* from inside the body of an exhibitionist, for I understand the pleasure of showing as intimately as the pleasure of watching. Perhaps the problem here *is* simply that Madonna's exhibitionism is being viewed as an economic strategy and a personality disorder, not just a sexual flavor. Then again, I have the distinct impression that Madonna's sexual exhibitionism is precisely what alienates the crowd.

As Susan Sontag said almost thirty years ago, there is only taste. Madonna's critics divide into two camps: those few who embrace Madonna as artist, as icon, and/or as object, and those who complain about being forced to look at *so many* pictures of her. It's a shame that these people got the review assignments; it's hard to get properly enthused about what you haven't sought out but rather are paid for—having *Sex* for money, so to speak. Perhaps this accounts for some of the flack Madonna has taken for remarking that porn models are not victims but exercise choice. How difficult to hear exhibitionism vindicated when you're feeling so dubious about your own voyeurism!

This brings me to another question: never mind if you jacked off. Did you actually enjoy looking at dozens of pictures—of *Madonna*? Or did the too-familiar face and the buffed butt drive you crazy? How can someone who sees no reason to abandon his or her vague distaste for what scholars are calling "The Madonna Phenomenon" ("Oh, God, *her* again") speak sensibly, much less profoundly, to a consumer who *wants* an album full of pictures of Madonna naked?

Funny how full the papers are of pronouncements: "The book is callous, callow, contrived." "It's joyless, hard, cold." "It's not art." (Now, a Mapplethorpe penis—what design! What balance!) Here in the sex community, where thoughtful and creative sex art has a small but hungry audience, people amused rather than repulsed by Madonna's slumming with piss-drinkers and punk lezzies with knives, flip the pages and say things like "Extraordinary." "Nice try." "Well, she did it."

Could it have been hotter? Sure, but maybe the other shoe has yet to drop. Remember, she signed a *two*-book contract.

I don't even know why I'm getting so exercised. I already knew that my and Madonna's culture vilifies sexually free women, S/M and leathersex, crossdressed women (even if they *are* Isabella Rossellini), and naked fags. Public response to *Sex* is not surprising; the surprise was the book itself, spading up the underground into chain bookstores for all the confused, fascinated, horrified world to see. Yeah, I know—Mapplethorpe already did it. But Mapplethorpe wasn't a woman, damn it. On the streets, in the clubs, in their scarf-festooned four-poster beds, sisters are scrutinizing the terra incognita of sex, mapping it both for pleasure jaunts and as a site for deep exploration. Most of the critics don't seem to understand (though some clearly do) that *Sex* comes with a sort of intellectual pedigree, or at least a recommended reading list. Maybe most of them haven't read *Caught Looking* or *Pleasure and Danger*. Would it come as a surprise to find out Madonna has?

Female and feminist sexual adventure produces its own theory, largely ignored by the media, which seems too invested in portraying feminists in general as anti-porn, even anti-sex. (The old agenda item "anti-male" also remains on the table.) These efforts to simplify and flatten a complex and fascinating debate inevitably stumble into the same trap photographer Meisel did with his ridiculous claim that after his, no one would ever have to produce another photoessay on eroticism. (How idiotic to say, "No one else needs to do a book of erotica"! *Everyone* ought to. How else do we begin to apprehend, if it is not shown and told, the full range of this culture's sex?) No one person—or faction of feminism—has a full vantage on sexuality; there can be no last word about it. Anyone who claims otherwise betrays arrogance or ignorance or both.

Sontag's essay "Notes on Camp" should have been on the re-

quired reading list for *Sex* critics, and in fact perhaps an advi-
sory label would have been in order: "Warning: Camp sensibility at play. Analyze accordingly." Madonna's whole career up to
and including *Sex* has depended heavily on campy imagery and
camp understandings of gender and sex. "The essence of Camp,"
says Sontag, "is its love of the unnatural: of artifice and exag-
geration." Many straight and feminist commentators have got-
ten lost in the translation and will continue to do so: when
Madonna insists that readers of *Sex* "who miss the humor are
missing a lot," it is this camp glee in presentation to which she
refers. But "Camp is esoteric—something of a private code,"
Sontag continues, and those who think they have nothing to
gain from sending up gender roles and hoary notions of "normal" sex may never crack it.

Further, "homosexuals, by and large, constitute the van-
guard—and the most articulate audience—of Camp." Without a
grasp of queer aesthetics (sexual and not, campy and not), it's
unlikely that reviewers could uncover either what's sexy about
*Sex* or what Madonnaphiles are likely to love. The poor things
are simply not coming to the project with a trained eye! It is an
affront—though a familiar one—when art produced through a
non-heterosexual lens is viewed as a freak show. Only the het-
ero-hegemony of this culture, which expects even homosexual
artists to conform to heterosexual themes, could produce in
*Vanity Fair* a cover story where writer Maureen Orth, white-
knuckled, informs us that "mainline heterosexual images are in
short supply" in *Sex*. Aside from one obvious response (for
which see the *Village Voice*'s Mim Udovich: to complain about
the lack of heterosexual images "is accurate only if you don't believe male-female s&m, sex with an older man, sex with a Bot-
ticellian younger man, biting a man's ass, shaving his pubic
hair, sucking on his toe, or sex with a man wearing makeup to
be heterosexual"), consider the impact of that statement on the
reader who sees (and notices that she or he sees) a weighty over-
abundance of heterosexual images outside the book's X-in-
scribed covers.

Madonna's queer community ties are not superficial, but
neither are they simple. Rather, a complicated web of reference

and affiliation ties Madonna to her audience, sometimes loosely, sometimes tightly. A gay community that would like to claim her puts more stock in the Sandra Bernhard factor than in her heterosexual relationships, then reads her gay male erotic references as rip-off: she steals from us! Another segment of the gay community simply responds viscerally to the images she mongers: she celebrates us! These communities would prefer to claim her only on their own terms; in the realm of identity politics, her identity is much too fluid for the gay community to view her as entirely trustworthy.

No, Madonna is a horse of another color, but only a culture of enforced poverty of sexual imagination would try to call her straight. In fact, the lesbian and gay communities' issues, insights, and agendas have spilled out of those communities' never-very-effectively-enforced boundaries and are now largely out of their control. So the spin Madonna puts on sexual liberation is a little too broad for the National Lesbian and Gay Task Force. Enter the queer community, which has surely influenced Madonna's thinking about sexual possibilities. Arguably, too, Madonna's prominence over the last decade has contributed to the cultural conditions which shaped the rise of the "new queerdom" itself. Here it's acceptable for girls to be boys and boys to be girls; here "lesbian" and "gay" are not the only alternatives to "straight."

Madonna, in fact, articulates the phenomenon of the queer het, the ostensibly straight person whose heterosexual persona covers a much more complicated sexual psyche. This is hardly a new sexual profile, but closet cases and swingers have historically taken no inspiration from the queer community. (Do I need to spell out that "bisexual" is the most self-evident word we might use to describe these non-gay non-hets? People resist the label, but good heavens, flip through *Sex* once more—it's illustrated by some powerful pictures.) Everybody has a sexuality—in fact, some people seem to have more than one—and the message of the gay community has at last begun to gain relevance for other segments of the populace, who think: if gays can fight to be respected and self-actualized around their sex, so can I.

Madonna uses her gay bar inspiration to chart other, less well known sexual arenas, but she never abandons her gay points of reference. Like queers, leatherfolk, and others, she's determined to live to tell. (Even when Madonna's songs themselves are anything but queer manifestoes, on the dance floor we pick out phrases that speak to us in the secret parallel language queers have always heeded: "Hope I live to tell the secrets I have learned," "Papa, don't preach," "You just keep on pushin' my love over the borderline.")

Straight men aren't the audience Madonna aims to address; no wonder so many of them don't like her. They'd be glad to fork over money if they felt she was *looking* at them, maybe even that she was styling herself with their particular gaze in mind. Ironically, though, the woman whose supposed pandering to men outraged so many feminists is really dressing up and performing for a mirror, and here again her queer and camp sensibilities get in the way of her being a traditional male's traditional object of traditional desire. Look at the Brassai-inspired photo spread she did for *Rolling Stone* (hardly a queer journal) where she's in your face with Weimar-era homosex and genderbend. No wonder the usual comment I hear from the straight-man-on-the-street is, "She doesn't do anything for me." If she does, he's probably dreaming of kissing her shoes, like the lucky hunk in *Sex*.

Taking all this into account, perhaps it's not so surprising that the other critics didn't join me in sticking their hands in their pants. Who knows how rare and rarefied this kink-soaked Madonnasex is, anyway? And thanks to our culture's tendency to marginalize sexual differences, how likely is it that the critics really want to help us find out?

So we have to become our own sexual intelligentsia. What makes me such an authority on Madonna? A ten-year-old girl who compared me to her started me on my career. More than one commentator on *Sex* has worried about the increasingly degenerate example Madonna is to the little girls who idolize her; if we can't convince each other that sexy pictures are bad for adults, surely we can agree that they're bad for kids.

But I've got news for them. I think kids like Madonna precisely *for* her sexuality, presented in strokes so bold that it's recognizable even to a child who hasn't yet been schooled in subtlety. When I was a child my favorite grownup was a friend of my mom's who differed from her in every conceivable way, and when I was an adult and viewed old photos of her I realized she was an absolute classic fifties sexpot. When I responded to her, and when my ten-year-old friend responds to me—or to Madonna—we're picking up on a vibe that resonates where hormones meet self-image. Today the message she intuits is one of self-actualization, not self-defeat. Who responds to eroticism more viscerally—and unconsciously—than a pubescent kid? When I ask my young friend and her pals what they like about Madonna, they chorus, "She's pretty!" Will they grow up to be Isabella Rossellinis in tweed coats?

I guess most grownups would rather they didn't. But better that than Allistair, tattooed and knife-wielding, eh? How dare Madonna suggest there are alternative ways of being women? And how many little girls are awaiting that news?

If the little boys are paying attention, they will surely see on display some very alternative ways of being men. This is all bound to drive the Christian Family folks insane, but I am here to tell you—when queer kids stumble upon *Sex*, it may well save some lives.

Little girls, little boys, and me: all of us want Madonna to take us there. (It's just this quality that was absent in most of the criticism of *Sex*.) It helps that, for me, the territory is familiar, and sex has a language that I know and work with all the time. Dream, fantasy and image are staples for me as a sex writer and sex worker; throw in the fact that Madonna pushes open communication (re-read the lyric sheet to "Justify My Love" if you doubt it) and you have the basics of sex therapy, as a few critics noted—though, absurdly, they could only come up with Dr. Ruth with whom to compare her.

Not that I have no criticisms of my own. Madonna works largely in image; I work mostly in words. I wish she'd pushed herself all the way to the wall for the written segments in *Sex*. I want what she knows (which seems visible in the collaborative images) to be said in words as boldly as it's said in pictures. Her words match the pictures' power only once, when her persona Dita says to her shrink, "Every time anyone reviews anything I do, I'm mistaken for a prostitute." Here camp meets sex-radical feminist theory, though I couldn't find a single reviewer who so much as noticed. The rest of the text has more in common with the pop songs that preceded it; whole pages of *Sex* reappear on the accompanying CD single "Erotica." This gives a Sensurround flavor to the project, but it doesn't much elevate its literary quality.

Much as I wish that the "Vogue" video had been made by Jennie Livingston, if not a videographer with roots in the drag balls (is *that* too naïve a desire?), I wish that Madonna were less glib in her appropriations. I'm not the first to say this—Dave Ford in San Francisco's lesbian/gay/bi *Bay Times* noted that Madonna had "consciously and vocally worked an intense gay agenda," but opined that her "symbiotic exchange" with the gay community "feels worn out now." Cindy Patton's analysis ("Embodying Subaltern Memory: Kinesthesia and the Problematics of Gender and Race") addresses this as well, though she notes that Madonna's appropriations also present alternative, useful images to other subsets of the culture. Indeed, I think this is what makes Madonna a phenomenon (for study, for cultural criticism) rather than only a wildly successful pop superstar—though, of course, she is that, too.

For me, Madonna goes too far occasionally: her gratuitous comments about fat people are weirdly situated in a work like *Sex*; likewise her spasm of homophobia in the Johnny letters seem a hedge against *really* going too far. S/M, abuse, feminism and porn are weighty subjects, and it's not surprising that most commentators find Madonna's light touch here insulting. As reviewer after reviewer went ballistic, I thought, "I think I know what you were trying to get at, Madonna, but it'd probably have been better to just keep it to yourself."

Mostly, though, I think she doesn't go far enough. What do I want, the moon? In fact, I do. I'm in close enough communication with my culture's reality, however, to know it won't be given to me by a star—and certainly not in a format I can buy in B. Dalton. Madonna isn't *un*-radical, but she *is* a pop artist. If she went "far enough" we'd never have seen her work, certainly not complete with media blitz and conglomerate-driven purchasing push.

I'd have picked a much sexier dog.

If in the end Madonna's *Sex* proves to be no more than the illustrated catalog to Nancy Friday's *My Secret Garden* (on second thought, make that *Women On Top*), it will still have accomplished something we see too little of: it will have made women's sexual imagination front page news. It will have taken some very queer images into mainstream media. It will have made us talk about sex.

The book's cultural importance does not lie chiefly in its artistic merit; its success (or failure) at portraying eroticism is not the point, nor is the "kinkiness" of the eroticism it portrays. Let's hope that the reviews of *Sex* have illustrated at least one thing: casting a critical (and, in most cases, untrained) eye on somebody else's sexual vision is an endeavor doomed to fail. It fails so dismally that I suspect most commentators don't even recognize that they are trapped in a deep cultural sinkhole. "It's not erotic" is a pronouncement so closely related to "It's not normal" that I'm almost embarrassed to see it repeated so often in print: the results of this Rorschach are all too clear. Americans—at least American book reviewers—aren't ready to embrace this much pluralism.

Evidently, though, Americans are willing to go into B. Dalton and plunk money down for a front row seat at the dialogue, and that's where I think *Sex*'s importance lies. Madonna, at the height of her cultural visibility, has used her stardom and her own skin to dare us to look squarely at sex. Sure, she's getting rich in the process, but anyone who maintains that that's all she intended has given the erotic content of *Sex* only a cursory glance, or no glance at all. *Sex* sells because it takes the edge off our unfulfilled hunger, it responds to our curiosity, it feeds our desire to be moved. Madonna invented none of this; her sexual imagination clearly fires her work, and the public's response to her is fired by the complex interplay between her personae, her willingness to explore sex publicly, and her fans' and viewers' own sexual yearnings and antipathies.

Madonna has intervened, very splashily and perhaps a little gracelessly, in a culture where dialogue about sex is still expected to be hushed, prurient, clinical, or—at its most outspoken—relegated to "alternative" venues. The importance of *Sex* lies in its appearance in chain bookstores, its superstar creatrix, its presence on the front page. Riding a wave generated by our need to talk about sex at least long enough to coax a condom onto a penis, Madonna—who has been a high-profile safe sex ambassador for years—has the nerve to talk about pleasure and variety, not risk groups and germs.

Hers is not the only voice in the dialogue, perhaps not even the loudest and certainly not the most sophisticated. But for a moment she had everyone's ear, and what she talked about was pleasure. Fantasy. Exploration. Polymorphous identities. Fetish sex.

Add these to the vocabulary we use to talk about *Sex*.

# Chameleon, Vampire, Rich Slut

*"You don't know if you want to hit me or kiss me."*
—Madonna

In an interview which appeared in the *Advocate* in 1991, Madonna addressed her now-fizzled relationship with Sandra Bernhard, saying:

> Whether I'm gay or not is irrelevant. I'm perfectly will-
> ing to have people think that I did [fuck her]...I don't
> care. If it makes people feel better to think that I slept
> with her then they can think it. And if it makes them
> feel safer to think that I didn't, then that's fine too.

Madonna is probably the only one ever to doubt the "relevance" of her sexuality to her audience. With the appearance of *Sex*, one can perhaps expect that she will stop making statements to this effect. Indeed, the central theme of the book is the exposure of Madonna's sexual secrets. Each page we turn will, we hope, uncover one of her heretofore unacknowledged and fabulously perverse pleasures. If we're lucky, those perversions will tap our own peculiar reservoirs of sexual tastes. But I think many of us approached the book intent upon collecting some more *knowledge* about Madonna's dirty secrets, rather than with the expectation that it might serve as the kind of book one reads with one hand. (Not that she made this kind of a read possible for us in such a cumbersome and sharp-edged format.) "Know-ing" Madonna is one of the primary pleasures involved in con-suming her. The more she reveals about herself, the more we want and the more we like wanting it. At least this is the way

I'm imagining Madonna's public image to operate for many of her queer fans who have been waiting to receive more juicy tidbits about her allegedly lesbian leanings since she appeared on *Late Night with David Letterman* with Sandra Bernhard in 1988.

Fortunately for us, the star has been more forthcoming with such tidbits for the past couple years. "Justify My Love" and *Truth or Dare* offered explicit suggestions of Madonna's sexual interests in other women. And to further satisfy our desire for Madonna's "real life" secrets, the documentary, "truth-telling" ethos of *Truth or Dare* encouraged a literal reading. We knew, finally, where some female fingers had been. But we hardly needed this "evidence" in order to make these connections long before Madonna ever made them for us. I was already imagining where *her* fingers had been when I saw her fall out of the sky and into the arms of the grinning gospel singer in the video "Like a Prayer." And the skinny, short-haired woman in drag who occupied a viewing booth to watch Madonna's peepshow rendition of "Open Your Heart" also served as a provocative clue.

For queer female viewers in particular, desire is the impetus behind this clue-seeking "read" of Madonna. In desiring her, we want to be able to imagine that she desires us right back. We want to know that *she* knows we're watching with desire; that acknowledgment would validate our affection for her and our lust for women more generally. One image that comes to mind, and which clearly suggests this pleasure, served as a promo shot for *Truth or Dare*. The photograph displays Madonna's bare back. Drawn upon her in black is the shape of a backstage pass which reads "All Access." Like the book *Sex*, Madonna's "rockumentary" *Truth or Dare* played on our voyéuristic pleasures and the pleasures involved in the illusion of acquiring some "truths" about Madonna's private life. But what's fun about the notion of "all access" isn't only the "access" we think we're being given. The fun also resides in the "all" so seductively inscribed upon her body. The inclusiveness implied by that "all" positions Madonna's female admirers in an openly sexual relationship to her, albeit in the form of a wish.

Madonna's appearance on the episode of *Saturday Night*

*Live* immediately following the inauguration of Bill Clinton provides yet another example of Madonna's sexual invitation to other women. In a skit meant to parody Marilyn Monroe's performance of "Happy Birthday, Mr. President," Madonna, dressed like Monroe, sings "Happy Inauguration, Mr. President" to Bill, Hillary, their daughter Chelsea, and the inaugural audience. Madonna's performance plays on the excessive seductiveness with which Monroe executed her performances as it recalls the historical narrative in which Monroe attempts to seduce John F. Kennedy. Therefore, as Madonna seductively gyrates and winks, and Bill (quite violently) attempts to prevent the angry Hillary from seeing her gestures, we are led to assume that Madonna intends to seduce Bill. But when Bill mouths the words, "You, me, later" and "I'll call you" to Madonna, she shakes her finger at him, mouthing back, "No, not you." "YOU," she mouths, as she points to Chelsea, who gulps and gestures to herself in disbelief, "ME?" "Yes, you," concludes Madonna. Like "all access," this performance comically demands that we look upon Madonna's performances as existing, not only (or even primarily) for straight male titillation, but also for the benefit of queer women. Monroe's transformation into Madonna thus gets "perverted": we witness the transformation of a woman, popularly constructed as desperately heterosexual, into a woman constructed as shamelessly queer. In this way, Madonna constructs herself as both the object and the subject of female desire.

The producers (and the critics) of pornography and commercial photography have long known how to create images which strongly signify the sexual availability of women to men. But Madonna's empire of images and interviews work not only to suggest her availability to men, but also to acknowledge and encourage the varied sexual desire of her (I would guess, largely) female and gay audience. In a word, this is groundbreaking. After all those years of wondering why the images of women produced by the fashion industry or by the Harlequin Corporation for female consumers are so damn sexually inviting, Madonna has finally outed a basic truism: straight or gay, consciously or not, many women are sexually attracted to other women.

Madonna's homoeroticism is particularly provocative given the more general way that questions of "authenticity" (i.e. of Madonna's "true" propensities) figure in the reception of her work. *Sex* has been touted everywhere and by Madonna herself as an earnest chronicle of the star's own sexual fantasies. What could be more private? More confessional? On the *Arsenio Hall Show*, Rosie O'Donnell chided Madonna about the absurd logical outcome of her exhibitionist, public self-exposures; in her hilarious reworking of the lyrics to "Vogue," O'Donnell joked (in song) that next we would see pictures of Madonna's "lungs and spleen." Foregoing her actual guts, Madonna does invite us to get ourselves beneath her skin via sexual fantasy. We are being allowed to go "deep inside" the real Madonna, journey-to-the-center style.

Nevertheless, our search for "true" signs of queerness in Madonna's image often disappoints. Madonna may be disclosing or confessing to us her "real" fantasies. But in so doing, she already defers the question of "reality" or "truth." After all, what could be more oxymoronic than the idea of a "real" fantasy? Fantasy is, by definition, that which exists outside the real (and purposefully so). Perhaps fantasy can become the "real" in the sense that it can be performed in a premeditated fashion. But in what sense are we to believe that these photographs and texts "authentically" represent the intricate machinations of Madonna's imaginary? Does she really fantasize about Vanilla Ice (whom she recruited to the project for his "kitsch value")? Need I say more?

Madonna herself points to this contradiction in the anxious preamble to *Sex* when she insists that "these are fantasies I have dreamed up" and later that "nothing in this book is true. I made it all up." Here, Madonna works against the ideologies of "realness" and "truth" deployed in the marketing of *Sex*. In effect, Madonna is pulling our metaphorical chains: she asks us to come up closer, go in deeper (and deeper) into the "real" woman, and simultaneously pulls us out—coitus interruptus— to restore us to her ("Dita's") "fantasies." Madonna's seduction thus moves in a continuous in-out-in-out rhythm. For many of her fans, especially those of us who are queer, her deployment of fantasy as a way of distancing herself from the stigma of the queer sexual practices she depicts is extremely disappointing.

This essay is an attempt to chart some of these (potential) pleasures and disappointments for Madonna's queer audience(s). In the process, I want to pay special attention to Madonna's self-representations of a particular kind of queer sexuality—bisexuality—as well as her critics' characterizations of her in "bisexual" terms. I do so hoping that I might reveal some of the political implications of wanting to "hit" or "kiss" Madonna. And perhaps I will go a little bit of the way toward understanding why we can't seem to decide which act is more satisfying.

First, we need to consider how the authenticity we look for in Madonna's image works paradoxically against the backdrop of her refusals to be "real" in any way. Beyond the pleasures involved in searching for clues to the secret of who Madonna really is, there is also a pleasure involved in knowing who she isn't. For feminist fans, the latter pleasure can be particularly powerful. Madonna and her press often mention feminists, but they usually do so wondering why feminists haven't yet realized Madonna's revolutionary potential to advance women's causes. Since that question never receives an answer, the audience is left to assume that feminism has reared its ugly humorlessness once again. But despite the critics' unwillingness to notice, many feminists have long been celebrating Madonna's "genderfuck" tactics. We (feminists) have long recognized that her excessive, campy, overtly theatrical performances of culturally intelligible female sexual styles have the potential to weaken naturalized notions of "woman." Furthermore, we have recognized that Madonna's powerful connection of female sexuality to a brazen, arrogant and in-your-face potency can be both personally empowering and loads of fun.

Similarly, many people have appreciated Madonna's forays into gay subcultural styles and her self-presentation as a woman who desires (and who is desired by) other women. In so doing, she complicates stable notions of heterosexuality and promotes gay life. Madonna messes with the authenticity and "naturalness" conferred upon heterosexuality in such a way as to encourage others to question the stability of their own heterosexual identities. I personally have known more than a few formerly "heterosexual" women for whom—I suspect—Madonna served as an enticement to "coming out" queer; perhaps now the "wannabe" has become the "wanna."

So Madonna can be lovable precisely because she produces herself as artificial, as that which can never be "known": her "self" is purely a product of cinema, fashion and pornography. Madonna doesn't exactly come off as a "heterosexual woman," but as a "heterosexual...NOT!, woman...NOT!" She said as much about herself in her campy 1991 address during MTV's ten year anniversary. After having burped, farted and spat for an international audience, Madonna characterized herself as follows: "She's a freak.... She's a man in drag. Just kidding. I'm a woman in drag. (Laughter) I'm a man and a woman. I'm your worst nightmare." Through her playful destabilizations of gender and sexual identity, she encouraged her audience to enjoy the same transgressions.

The double move Madonna makes as she promises "truths" and delivers "untruths" has long been the central and defining aspect of her work. But questions of truth and untruth, authenticity and inauthenticity become very problematic when one considers the way in which bisexuality figures into Madonna's sexual ethos. We don't know the nature of Madonna's favorite sexual practices or the sex of her partners, past or present. And even if we could decide that Madonna is "truly" bisexual, thus conferring a stroke of authenticity upon her, it would be fruitless. Bisexuality is already caught up in ideologies of inauthenticity and stereotypes of opportunism and sexual excess. In choosing to "flirt" with bisexuality, Madonna therefore enters into yet another web of confusion about knowing, identity, and truth-telling.

Whatever else it does, *Sex* represents the clearest articulation of bisexuality in Madonna's work to date. Whether or not we read the book literally as evidence of Madonna's bisexuality, it does attempt to construct Madonna, the sexual persona, as a "bisexual." For queer audiences, this representation of bisexuality works in some fairly problematic ways. It's true that

Madonna's mainstreaming of gay images has great liberatory potential and encourages mass acceptance of homosexuality. However, the production of Madonna's "bisexuality" (in her own work and in her critics' descriptions of it) also contributes to negative perceptions of bisexuals who are often seen as inauthentic sexual opportunists.

Bisexuality seems to have a lot to offer popular culture. In narrative film, it makes for plot-twisting characters. Bisexuals are unpredictable, excessively sexual, and essentially unstable—or so the story goes. Their objects of desire may change with such rapidity that it seems impossible to pin that desire down, to define it. Thus, for those who cling to stable identity categories, the phrase "bisexual identity" would seem to be an oxymoron. Identity suggests singularity, while bisexuality suggests a chameleon-like ability to transform into something else. *Basic Instinct*, a film which capitalized on the potential that a bisexual character affords a Hollywood plot, has shown us that bisexuality communicates these themes. The character Catharine Tramell, played by Sharon Stone, provides the plot with just the right ingredients for blockbuster mystery/suspense film: instability, uncertainty, promiscuity, and danger. We can't really know her character because we can't pin down her sexual desires. Her bisexuality makes her so elusive that we can't even determine, down to the last moment, whether or not she is capable of murder. And so the film ends with a question mark, the emblem of bisexuality.

Unfortunately, the same question mark around bisexuality has currency in queer communities, making it difficult for many women and men who do not define themselves on the basis of sexual object choice to feel at home there. In a recent issue of *Genre*, a bisexual writer complains that bisexuals are "mistrusted by homos because we're seen as traitorous chameleons who get our kicks with them and then go off to live our white-picket-fence dream and [to] curse faggots." (Publications like *Bi any Other Name* [Alyson Press] and a magazine called *Anything That Moves* participate in an effort to dispel many of these notions.) Not surprisingly, *Sex* similarly adopts some fairly unappealing constructions of bisexuality in order to create

Madonna's exotic and excessive sexuality. For example, the handwritten letters between Madonna's sexual persona, Dita, and her male lover, Johnny, best exemplify this representation of bisexuality as excessive, insatiable, promiscuous and ultimately male-centered. The story begins in Cannes where Dita vacations naked in the sun with her female lover, Ingrid. Dita writes to Johnny about the sheer man-hungry horniness of the two women:

> I wish I could stop playing with myself and thinking about sex. I'm gonna have to go now cause I have to finger fuck Ingrid or she's gonna freak. It's the only way to get her away from the edge. Really! Hurry and come over here with some other forms of entertainment for me and the lovely Ingrid.

Here, and throughout the letters, Dita and Ingrid appear voraciously, pathologically hungry for sex with multiple partners. Usually, the two women seem largely uninterested in each other, except insofar as they interact with Johnny, who must save the two women from the apparent boredom and non-climactic nature of lesbian sex. When Dita learns that Johnny is also having gay sex, she is not merely jealous, but downright homophobic in her response. She dumps Johnny in a letter which explains:

> I haven't told Ingrid yet. I'm not sure how she's gonna take it. Mayby [sic] she'll feel better knowing her competition isn't another woman. As for me, I think I'm gonna be sick. Next time you want pussy, just look in the mirror.

This construction of female bisexuality is common in mainstream heterosexual porn for male audiences. There, the bisexual woman serves as a signifier of the sexually perverse in such a way as to excite the male heterosexual viewer (who may consume two writhing female bodies at once) and yet avoid being implicated in any connotations of gay sexuality. Dita's repulsion at Johnny's homosexual practices serves to underscore this particular construction of bisexuality.

Madonna does not in fact claim the label of bisexuality for herself. On the contrary, she keeps her public image at arm's length from this and any other sexual label. In the many interviews she has done, the question of her sexual relationship to other women inevitably emerges. Consider the following conversations:

Q: Which do you prefer?
M: Which kind of sex do I prefer? Hetero sex.
Q: But you also like the other kind as well?
M: It's not, Do I like the other kind as well? I have a lot of sexual fantasies about women, but by and large I'm mostly fulfilled by being with a man.
Q: But you can also be fulfilled by being with a woman sometimes?
M: It's not the same.

Q: You've never explicitly said in the media you've had lesbian experiences in reality, have you?
M: Yes.
Q: Yes, you have? When was that?
M: I don't think that's important. Why don't you ask me about my heterosexual experiences?

What becomes clear in these exchanges is Madonna's reluctance to reveal anything about herself that might attach stigma to her very successful career. And yet she is also extremely careful not to *completely* disassociate herself from the cachet that her affiliation with gay sexuality affords: "If it makes people feel better" to believe that she's having gay sex, then that's good; but "if it makes them feel safer" to think that she has not, then "that's fine too." Since Madonna wants to attract both gay audiences and mainstream heterosexual audiences, she constructs a sexuality which is "safe" for both audiences (thus giving a whole new meaning to the term, "safe sex"). This kind of inclusivity can be infuriating to gay audiences who want to see her more committed to gay politics and less interested in seducing straight men. A pessimistic, though compelling, response might be that Madonna's "safe" bisexual persona is a matter of cross-audience appeal, a clever marketing ploy, a cheap trick.

But I don't want to completely resign my long-standing membership in the fan club, so I'd like to qualify this last comment: it fails to dispute the image of bisexuality as a kind of sexual opportunism often conflated with an almost universally reviled sense of economic opportunism. When we characterize Madonna as bisexual-for-the-sake-of-capitalist-gain, we climb into a huge bed with a veritable orgy of strange—and boring—bedfellows.

In the mainstream press, the fashion magazines, and the gay press there seem to be two main charges often leveled at Madonna; both accuse her of some form of inauthenticity. The first charge, which seems to emerge from a variety of different political quarters (though still largely from within the mainstream press), addresses Madonna's wealth: she's greedy for money, they say. The second charge is often made in the gay press (only to be quickly rescinded): Madonna is guilty of "appropriating" the regalia of gay and lesbian subcultures. This critique assumes that Madonna herself resides outside of those communities and must in effect steal their styles, symbolisms, and rituals. These notions—"opportunism" and "greed"—have *long* been major themes in Madonna's reception by both the mainstream and the gay press.

Those two objections dovetail: "appropriation" is a strategy which serves as an expression of opportunistic economic greed. That is, Madonna's critics often make an interesting set of connections between appropriation, greed, and sexuality, relying upon a suspicion of bisexuality. What I'm suggesting is that Madonna has long been constructed by her critics in the mainstream press (even before *Sex, Truth or Dare,* or "Justify My Love") by means of the sexphobic, homophobic, and "biphobic" symbolism associated with bisexuality. Thus, to stand in their camp bemoaning Madonna's inauthenticity, greed, and opportunism, is to risk employing and encouraging these negative perceptions of bisexuality. One therefore needs to use caution in employing these notions, if not to avoid them altogether.

But I do not wish to summarily condemn all attempts to construe Madonna's work as "appropriative." For instance, the notion of "appropriation" is necessarily central to arguments about Madonna's uses of "blackness" to foreground her very pale "whiteness," thus absorbing and displacing racial "otherness." (I am thinking here in particular of bell hooks's essay about Madonna in her book *Black Looks*.) I do not wish to dispute this characterization of Madonna's work as "appropriative." Rather, my point is that the popular strategy of equating Madonna with a voracious sexual appropriativeness construes her in homophobic ways; in effect, critics use notions long associated with deviant sexualities to covertly punish Madonna for her sexual "deviations." Most critics of her appropriation fail to address the concrete abuses of power which take form in Madonna's representations of her own sexuality in relation to African American and Latino (queer) sexualities.

When it comes to talking about Madonna, suddenly everybody is a critic of capitalism. Critics of Madonna's fortune and of Madonna-as-capitalist come out of the woodwork in the most unlikely places. *The National Review* scorned Madonna in a cover story in 1991 after her Blond Ambition tour. (It wasn't enough for them to give her a snide review. Madonna's face appears on the cover with her eyeballs scratched out, looking like the product of someone's high school tantrum.) As in many other popular analyses of Madonna's fame, this scornful response involves damning her with faint praise for her "business acumen." *The National Review* accuses Madonna of having acquired "a keen sense of whom it's profitable to offend and whom it isn't." Similarly, *Entertainment Weekly* describes Madonna as a "dollarwise diva" who's an expert at "media manipulation." Even better, *Vanity Fair's* 1990 cover story characterizes her as "that perfect hybrid that personifies the decadently greedy, selfishly sexual decade that spawned her—a corporation in the form of flesh." Madonna herself has acknowledged the existence of this kind of criticism, describing it as "an insult in the form of a compliment."

Perhaps it is not surprising that few people can mange to leave unremarked the fact that Madonna *sells* sex. We aren't supposed to approve of sex for money. Neither are polite folk supposed to look approvingly at the sale or consumption of pornography. All of this explains the *grudging* acknowledgment of Madonna's economic success. To describe her as a "corporation in the form of flesh" is most telling (and most strange) because it joins the sexual "greed" we associate with sixties sexual liberation and the economic greed we associate with present-day corporate culture. In this description, Madonna appears as a "hybrid" of these two kinds of greed: a rich, horny, "sexually liberated" prostitute who loves her work. What could be more monstrous? When Madonna's sexuality isn't being subsumed in a discussion of her marketing bravado, it is being protested for its narcissism. Either way, rapacity is the underlying characteristic which everyone must ascribe to her.

The "appropriative" quality of Madonna's work also creates a lot of discomfort amongst her critics. *New Statesman and Society* has characterized her work the most harshly in this regard, arguing that it "smacks of colonialism" both in its race politics and in the way that it "uses homosexual provocation to get suburban America and Europe stampeding to the movie houses." In the gay press especially, there is a concern over her motives in appropriating gay subcultural codes and styles. In an article for *Gay Community News*, Sydney Pokorny writes:

> Madonna is especially adept at transposing the culture codes of subcultural groups into mass culture. She adorns herself with the markings of the Other and then sells that look to the masses through the wanna-be phenomenon....She is a double agent who sells out to the other side.

But despite what would seem like a clear discomfort with the politics of Madonna's adoption of gay cultural codes, Pokorny, like other gay writers, ultimately forgives Madonna: "Although this is clearly an appropriation of our culture and our aesthetic, it is not all bad." With Pokorny and many other gay critics, this kind of ambivalence is common. However, these critics often (perhaps temporarily or provisionally) resolve this ambivalence in the last instance through a celebration of her image. For them, it is politically more important to celebrate the sexual and gender transgressions which Madonna introduces into popular culture than to slam her for being capitalist or for not being original, authentic, or even "Other" enough.

The popular press likewise expresses ambivalence about Madonna—not in order to celebrate gender and sexual transgressions, but to vent latent hostility towards (and probably also fear of) her. There, Madonna's appropriations of the styles of gay subculture as well as the styles of vintage Hollywood stars like Marilyn Monroe are often characterized quite enthusiastically as nothing less than monstrous. In two different cover stories/interviews which appeared in *Vanity Fair* (1990) and *Vogue* (1992), Madonna appears as a vampire. Kevin Sessums quotes an unnamed member of Madonna's entourage who claims that Madonna "sucks what she needs out of somebody, then moves on to the next set of victims." Sessums later comments that since Madonna has "surrounded herself" with Sandra Bernhard and Warren Beatty, "she must be sharpening those teeth down to a nice set of fangs." Likewise, and with even more forthrightness, David Handelman gets down to this point in the *Vogue* interview. He writes:

> But like a vampire, Madonna continually renews herself by drawing strength from others—not just her collaborators, but her audience. She has a powerful need to mess with people's heads, as well as other body parts.

Both authors execute their articles with a great deal of ambivalence about the star; both features flatter Madonna even as they describe her as a bloodsucker.

Whenever critics make reference to Madonna's role as the "Great Appropriator," they inevitably end up in a discussion of the "constant genesis" of Madonna's (appropriated) image. Thus, not only is she seen as a vampire, but she is also often likened to a "chameleon," which changes its skin to suit its

environment and which has no "true" colors of its own. The
image of the chameleon brings us back around to notions of
(in)authenticity, greed, marketing...and, of course, bisexuality.
The implicit question behind all of these images of Madonna is:
who is she, really? Who is the "real" person, Madonna? And the
implicit answer: she's a fake. She falsely adopts these sexual
personae in order to make obscene amounts of money. Once
Madonna's artificiality has been established, it is easy to proceed down a slippery slope: in taking on these excessively sexual personae, different from one month to the next, Madonna is
not even a "real" woman. When you ask her what her name is,
she's the girl who responds, "what do you want it to be?" She's
scarcely even human; in her hard-bodied health (or illness, depending on which magazine you read), she's machinic, corporate; she's an animal or monster. Or, in Joyce Brothers's heart-
felt terms, she's simply a "rich slut." (So much for the feminist
utopia imagined in Madonna's transgressive deconstructions of
womanhood.)

The images of Madonna I've described here betray a frus-
tration with the inability to know her, to identify her—sexually
or otherwise. They show us that it's infinitely easier (and more
politically palatable to neocon America) to conclude that she's a
"fake" than to contend with the larger implications of this frus-
tration (such as the acceptance of womanhood and heterosexuality as cultural—and not biological—mandates). Therefore,
Madonna's critics mobilize ideologies of economic and sexual
greed in order to characterize her in less-than-flattering terms
in even the most favorable reviews of her performances. A complicated female bisexuality which is aggressive, demanding,
self-loving, and even parodic of heterosexuality, must be forced
to lose face somehow. In Madonna's case, it means that we
must view this potent sexuality as exploitative.

In the popular imagination, bisexuality is a threat which
needs to be stamped out. Like Catharine Tramell of *Basic Instinct*, Madonna is to be understood as a lecherous thing which
exploits its victims and leaves them when its has no use for
them any more. Likewise, conservative, violently homophobic
minds have likened bisexuals to vampires in order to construct

them as the dangerous "link" between the "diseased" gay community and "healthy" heterosexuals. These homophobic images also find their way into the gay community, where the most prominent anti-bisexual image is that of the "traitorous chameleon," who is not "authentically" gay but may appear so. Another dangerous character.

Madonna herself deploys some of the cultural codes which cast bisexuals as psychologically unstable, greedy people. But long before she herself made that blunder, her critics were busily creating a sex-phobic, bisexual ethos around her. They have adopted all the cultural metaphors which signal this particular form of sexual danger. In their descriptions of her life and work, they have emphasized the central accusations which bigots use to denigrate bisexuals: opportunism, inauthenticity, exploitation, and greed.

Several interesting questions arise here. Broadly speaking, why do the few available terms used to critique capitalism mobilize images of "deviant" bisexuality? To what extent might capitalism itself have influenced the production of this sexuality/identity? Do sexual ideologies *often* serve as convenient red herrings, distracting from the real injustices of capitalism and conflating them with the "evils" of deviant sex? These questions must be left for another essay. But in the meantime we can notice that Madonna offers her conservative homophobic critics the opportunity to put into play both of these overlapping systems of meaning. Her critics will therefore repeatedly argue that she is economically opportunistic, exploitative and greedy, and then they will argue that her opportunism is a product of her excessive, greedy (bi)sexuality. Greed slides quite easily back and forth between two terms: sex and money.

As both a critic and a fan of Madonna, as a feminist, and as a committed advocate of gay/lesbian/bisexual rights, I find myself in a labyrinth. I do not think that an unconditional celebration of Madonna's work is a good political choice. We must point the finger when she is the source of damaging, homophobic and "biphobic" images and actions as well as the source of problematic representations of race and class. But it is equally important to recognize that many of our own objections to her have already been set into play in a maze of cultural meanings which connect a queer sexuality—bisexuality—to images of greed and corruption. We must therefore recognize when our criticisms of Madonna feed homophobic ideologies, when "hitting"—instead of "kissing"—her will also cause injury to ourselves and our queer communities.

*I would like to thank the following people for helping me to think through these issues: Linda Baughman, Lisa Duggan, Stacey Gross (Madonna's biggest fan ever), Maria Mastronardi, Bob Steltman, and, especially, Annette Van, who far exceeds Madonna on the "Babe" scale. Robobabe.*

PAT CALIFIA

# *Sex* and Madonna, Or, What Did You Expect from a Girl Who Doesn't Put Out on the First Five Dates?

I'm surprised that any real rock 'n' roll ever gets recorded, because the whole point of that relentless, remorseless beat is to get everybody's pants off, their skirts up, and their pelvises colliding like crazed refrigerator magnets. Not that the words don't matter, too. There's a reason why mothers and other vice cops are always bitching about not being able to understand the words. *If you knew what those goddamned kids were talking about, you'd scream like a scalded cat and pull the plug.* The lead singers of cutting-edge rock 'n' roll have a hundred ways to code, cover up, speed up, hint at, scratch, sample, shout, and otherwise protect their poetry of dispossession. Ever since the fifties, the virtue of rock was that it said or hinted at things you'd never see on television.

Now MTV has made it possible to mate transgressive imagery to the backbeat. In rock videos, quick cuts serve much the same purpose as a growled, half-heard, raunchy vocal—they obscure a thought crime, making it just marginally possible that the artist might get away with an upsetting message. It's no accident that the growing movement to censor rock 'n' roll can trace its origins back to the founding of MTV. New technologies are always used for sexual purposes, and any time a new, sexually-explicit form of media gets off the ground, new nabobs of censorship start sending out mass mailings to solicit funds to winnow out the bad seeds of Satan. It happened when the printing press was invented, when paperback books became popular in the fifties, when comic books were first produced, and when the rental of X-rated videocassettes took off. It's also no accident that the most recent explosion of politically and erotically charged popular music is firmly situated in the middle of a campaign against so-called child pornography. Kiddy-porn has become a buzzword. This particular moral panic is not really about protecting children, just as McCarthyism wasn't really about Communist infiltration of the army. It is about building a Berlin Wall between adults and teenagers, consolidating adult control over young people, and making it difficult or impossible for minors to live outside of or in opposition to their biological families, control their own sexuality, and create their own culture.

Rock 'n' roll has had a lot of very satisfying, shocking moments. Much of the sexual dialogue of rock has focused on S/M, homosexuality, gender transgression, and sex for pleasure instead of procreation. There was Mick Jagger (or somebody who sounded an awful lot like him) sneering, "Where can I get my cock sucked? Where can I get my ass fucked? I may have no money, but I sure know where to put it every time" in "Cocksucker Blues." There was Jim Morrison showing his audience exactly what they might find if they broke on through to the other side of his fly. Ostensibly heterosexual Jim Carroll's Catholic Boy smirked, "I put my tongue to the rail whenever I can," and in "Venus in Furs," then openly gay Lou Reed had some sinister things to say about archetypal male submissive Severin and his Whiplash girlchild in the dark. Of course, that was way back when, and Lou still deserved to have somebody kiss his shiny, shiny boots of leather. David Bowie's extended flirtatious shout to the "Rebel, Rebel" who "got your mother in a whirl, she's not sure if you're a boy or a girl...Hot tramp, I love you so," justified a generation that wanted to wear combat boots with their crinolines. More recently, Prince confidentially told his inamorato, "If your old man ain't no good, come on over to my neighborhood. We can jump in the sack, and I'll jack u off."

Women in rock have often had even nastier things to say than the plugged-in boys, especially when you consider their proportionally fewer numbers. Patti Smith's "Horses" is an ecstatic ballad about a boy being gang-banged in a locker room. Few of her fans know she was photographed both as a female punk rocker and a very realistic leatherman in the out-of-print S/M classic, Michael Grumley and Ed Gallucci's *Hard Corps* (E. P. Dutton, 1977). Chrissie Hynde's "Tattooed Love Boys" reads like a straight girl's tribute to rough trade ("I shot my mouth off, and he showed me what that hole was for"). Demolition Man Grace Jones did almost nothing but talk about sex ("Pull up to the bumper, baby, in your long black limousine"). The DiVinyls's Christina Amphlett took an aggressively independent stand about her libido ("Please don't ask me how I've been getting off...It's a fine line between pleasure and pain"), and Marianne Faithfull got very pointed with an unfaithful lover ("Every time I see your dick, I see her cunt in my bed"). Even the normally rather staid, albeit gender-fucking, art rocker Annie Lennox ground out an arch little piece about masochism ("I need someone to pin me down so I can live in torment...I need someone to crack my skull, I need someone to kiss").

Some people would probably quibble about labeling Madonna a rocker, but if your criterion for that label is someone who creates popular music with a hip-surging beat and lyrics that challenge middle-class, WASP sensibilities, there's no doubt that she belongs in the pantheon. She was one of the first music stars with mass appeal to realize how much potential there was for confrontation and social commentary in a rock video, and she is certainly the most astute when it comes to exploiting shock value commercially. The pundits cluck when she chains herself to a bed, dresses up her male dancers in big, fake, pointy tits, sings about a teenage mother who is not going to give up her baby, and kisses the feet of a black man unjustly accused of a crime (who later turns out to be Jesus). But the public keeps buying her records. So far, Madonna has been smart enough to turn every single attack on her to her advantage. When the cops threatened to bust her for obscenity during a concert, it simply gave her concert movie *Truth or Dare* a harder edge. When MTV yanked "Justify My Love" (after broadcasting it just often enough so everybody knew exactly what the fuss was all about), Madonna turned the blackout into a commercial for the gender-bending, softcore *noir* video, which became a best-seller. She went on *Nightline* in an I-am-not-a-bimbo business suit and kicked butt about safe sex and sex education. And it became very clear that somebody should write a song about the MTV brass along the lines of the Sex Pistols's "EMI."

It's hard to guess if the flap about *Sex*, its companion video and album, *Erotica*, and the movie *Body of Evidence* will make the Material Girl's bottom line even more impressive or serve as a grim marker for future biographers chronicling the Beginning of the End of her career. *Sex* has received tons of press. Unfortunately, like most things that are perceived as pornographic, the book has rarely been reviewed as a serious work within a specific social and political context. Most of the reviews don't tell you much about the book or about Madonna or even about sex, whether kinky or mundane. You learn only how the critic feels about S/M dykes, gay men, cross-generational sex, and notorious, bleached-blond women who make "too much" money. Most of these byliners make *Sex* sound like one of those elusive snuff movies that pornography abolitionists are always scaring the public with but never actually showing us.

Despite the hysterical claims of pop cult hand-wringers, this book is not obscene. Claims that it is pornography and ought to be banned are made out of ignorance of the law. You can bet every dollar you didn't spend on the book that Time-Warner had their legal beagles go over it with one of those combs your doctor gives you when you get a prescription for Kwell. There's a reason why you don't see any erect cocks in this book—the same reason why you don't see any penetration or anyone who even remotely resembles a minor. It's the same reason why the often-deplorable text was included. Everybody say, "socially redeeming value," now. That Mylar wrapping isn't just about making the reader participate in an act of violation to gain access to the contents—it's about protecting distributors from charges that they let kids look at it. *Sex* very carefully keeps a wide piece of the street between itself and the long arm of Lily Law. Some poor dumb bastard of a district attorney will be sure to drag *Sex* into court for being obscene and is equally sure to lose, especially going up against the resources of Time-Warner.

*Sex* is not violent. True, a knife appears in a few photos, but I hope I know the difference between a blade that's being wielded as a stage prop (Madonna's clothes don't even get torn, for heaven's sake) and one that's being used as an edged weapon. The most violent thing about *Sex* has been the indigestion professed by its detractors, and the deplorable things that boys in coffee shops have been talking about doing to Madonna because it's what that smartass, filthy-minded, back-talkin' bitch deserves.

Nevertheless, the book is undeniably kinky. The photographs in *Sex* include a lot more than S/M imagery. It is that material (and, to a lesser extent, the inclusion of lesbians and gay men) which has fueled the moralists' scorn. The response to *Sex* is in large part an index of how the guardians of norms and mores feel about bondage and discipline. Glad as I am to imagine baby pervs boosting a copy of *Sex* in Barnes & Noble, slitting it open with a switchblade in the nearest alley, and saying to themselves, "Lookie there, I'm not the only one," I think it's reasonable for those of us who live on the sexual fringe sans Steven Meisel's camera lens to ask Darling Dita the Dominatrix Diva, "Are you a good witch, or are you a bad witch?" Is the publicity the leather community is getting out of this book worth the backlash it will generate and the distortions it—and any mass-media image of fetish sex—contains?

The way Madonna deals with other sexualities does not bode well for her ability to pass S/M 101. The photographs of a childlike Madonna with a heavyset, older man present a wonderful opportunity to broaden consumers' stereotypical ideas about physical attractiveness and explicate fantasies about cross-generational sex and incest. Instead, Madonna delivers a stunningly stupid diatribe about fat people being "overindulgent pigs." Her pithy appraisal of women being "willing to accept a situation where the man is less attractive because of the who earns the bread situation" can't redeem this hateful statement. Madonna has defended this comment elsewhere as only her personal opinion, but it also seems to be the opinion of every high-fashion periodical and hardcore porn magazine I've ever seen. The most powerful and hip glamour queen in America can't dethrone anorexia. Pardon me, but I don't think I'll cancel my subscription to *Bear* magazine. I don't sleep with girls who can't pinch an inch. Some welts turn me on, but getting bruised by a pair of famished-looking hip bones is no fun at all. If I wanted to look at those kinds of bodies, I could join the Marines in Somalia. So pass me the mashed potatoes and gravy, would you, Dita?

The infamous page that begins, "Sex with the young can be fun," is mildly amusing. But most people are not going to get the joke. (How can a hairless, virgin boy give somebody crabs? Where the hell did *he* get them?) Our society expects young people to delay being sexually active for almost a decade after they reach puberty and punishes sexually active minors by denying them access to privacy, sex education, birth control, abortion, and treatment for STDs. Age-of-consent laws that are supposed to protect young people from being molested are actually used most often to punish adult gay men who make erotic connections with gay teenagers. The law-enforcement bureaucracy charged with enforcing our vague and draconian child pornography laws has become the only above-ground source for child pornography in this country, which it uses in a multitude of expensive and heartbreaking entrapment schemes that are patently unconstitutional. Instead of opening the door to a more intelligent discussion of any of these issues, Madonna's flippant comment simply makes her a big, fat target for the kiddy-porn witch finders.

This blend of innovative imagery and dunderhead commentary makes *Sex* a frustrating and baffling read. It's wonderful to see real lesbians in mainstream erotica. These tattooed, pierced, skinny, grinning girls with knives are miles away from the faux-dykes who populate most straight magazines—heavily made-up *Penthouse* pets with airbrushed boobs who are carefully posed so their tongues and pussies don't quite touch. The photograph of a reclining man with a mirror on his chest which is reflecting one of Madonna's breasts could be a poster for transgender liberation. And the ribald party that Madonna hosts at a gay-male burlesque house makes us wonder if fag hags weren't always getting a little more cock than their queer escorts would like you to believe.

But all this is offset by a nasty letter from Dita who is really pissed off about accidentally discovering her lover Johnny getting a blow job from his best friend, Ben. The letter closes, "I

think I'm gonna be sick. Next time you want pussy, just look in
the mirror. Gone fishing, Dita." This, from a girl who has had
Ingrid's face in her kipper snacks all through the book! This
doesn't read like parody or irony or a clever exposé of sexual
hypocrisy. It reads more like one of those disclaimers on a vibrator box: *Do not use over red or swollen skin. Sold for novelty
purposes only.* In other words, we were just kidding, folks, we
wanted to take your money, but this really isn't about sex at all.

During the fifties and much of the sixties, if you picked up
a book or saw a movie that had queer characters, you knew two
things: (1) they were going to be portrayed as freaks or villains
or both, and (2) they would be dead by the end of the story. If I
had a choice, I would rather have some mention of gay people
(however distorted) than no mention at all. It's important to recognize how many people would like to ban even these limited
and crippled images of same-sex love. But such double-edged
materials are the reason why activists need to mount anti-
defamation as well as anti-censorship campaigns. While these
stereotypes might alert a nascent gay or bi person to the fact
that "those people" really do exist, they also discourage the
viewer from acting on their queer desires by portraying them as
being inherently toxic, dangerous, and sick.

*Sex* is sprinkled with moments like the mandatory gay suicide scene in a fifties pulp novel—as if even Madonna had been
freaked out about going too far and had to show a wide streak
of conservatism to make the outlandish parts of the book more
palatable. Oh, well, she does say, "I'm not interested in porno
movies because everybody is ugly and faking it and it's just
silly. They make me laugh, they don't turn me on." So perhaps
it's wise to view *Sex* as a parody of pornography.

Madonna seems to get some of the basics about S/M being
safe, sane, and consensual. "There's something comforting
about being tied up," she says. And elsewhere—"I talked to a
dominatrix once and she said the definition of S & M was that
you let someone hurt you who you know would never hurt you."
She even says, "It's always a mutual choice...I don't even think
S & M is about sex. I think it's about power...."

But these tentative, tender buds of blossoming understanding are (sigh) wilted by some vile flatulence about battered women. "Some people want to be punished. Some women want to be slapped around...I think for the most part if women are in an abusive relationship and they know it and they stay in it, they must be digging it. I suppose some people might think that's an irresponsible statement." Well, yes. Of course there are some women who seem determined to stay with their violent partners. But this has nothing to do with S/M. Why drop it in the middle of the bondage photo spread? Madonna (and her handlers) seem to have no notion of the social forces that can shape or limit our ability to even imagine that we have choices, let alone give or withhold consent.

Many of the photos taken in the Vault are striking. I'm overjoyed to see this space and some of its denizens recorded here for posterity. These images are potentially as historically significant as the photos Brassai took in Parisian lesbian bars during the thirties and Ernest J. Bellocq's early twentieth century portraits of Storyville prostitutes. But I doubt that Madonna (or most of the people who read *Sex*) know or care about the struggle to keep S/M territory available in New York, San Francisco, and other cities. The Vault was called the Hellfire Club during the seventies, and it was closed during an AIDS panic that also resulted in the closure of the Mineshaft and a half-dozen other leather clubs and vanilla swing-party spaces. Campaigns to close the bathhouses also shut down most of the public space available to leather people in other urban areas.

The ostensible goal of those campaigns was to stop men from having unsafe sex with each other. In fact, it simply moved anonymous public sex into adult bookstores, tearooms, and rest stops, where there's no place to wash up, no place to get a condom, and very little time or social pressure to insist on latex barriers. It also increased the numbers of men arrested for lewd behavior and made them more vulnerable to getting bashed. When the baths closed, a major source of capital was cut off. This money had funded political activism, the arts, and other cultural activities. Gay-male bathhouses and S/M clubs also housed other sexual minorities. Just before the Mineshaft was padlocked, heterosexual and women-only parties were being held there. Other gay men's clubs in Manhattan had also hosted dyke sex parties. Leather dykes in Manhattan were not welcome at the Duchess, a dyke bar where you got served your drink in a dirty glass if the bartender thought you were a perv, so we took over corners of the straight dungeons. The Catacombs, the Caldron, and the Hothouse in San Francisco also opened their doors to mixed-gender or women-only events.

I feel deeply ambivalent about somebody who has not paid her dues using my community as a series of bizarre backdrops for a photo shoot. Leather bars, clubs, and dungeons are the places where fetishists and sadomasochists meet, relax, find new friends and lovers, play, and create a community. Many of these places are far from perfect. They are often fire hazards—Mafia-run, dirty, small, and overpriced. But without them we would be even more marginalized, even more isolated. We can never take this space for granted. We have to simultaneously defend, occupy, expand, guide others to, and hide our territory if we are going to survive as a people. I'm afraid *Sex* is going to attract more tourists and moral crusaders to the sexual underground than cognoscenti.

Any positive information about S/M which can be gleaned from the pages of *Sex* has to be considered along with the movie which was released along with it, *Body of Evidence*. Madonna plays a woman who is formally charged with murdering a wealthy elderly lover who has left her all his money. She claims she's being persecuted because of her appetite for domination, but it turns out she's just a gold-digging murderess after all. No, stop it, I never would have guessed. This movie belongs firmly in the same genre as *Cruising, Basic Instinct*, and a slew of B-flicks and true-crime TV shows that titillate viewers with as much fetish attire and kinky sex as the censors will allow, at the price of making a clear connection between murder and sadomasochism. The directors of this tripe all seem to be channeling Richard von Krafft-Ebing.

Watching Aesop's fables collide with <<*O*>> magazine would just be campy fun if it didn't have such negative consequences for pervs. Many of us never find others who share our erotic interests, or we delay our attempts to find the kinky com-

munity for years. Even when we get the courage to buy a latex
catsuit or a riding crop and play out our fantasies, we are ham-
pered by self-doubt and an unnecessary burden of fear because
there are so few positive images of sadomasochists. We get fired
from our jobs, evicted, hassled on the street, and we lose custody of our children because of stereotypes like these.

Sadomasochists' First Amendment rights are under fierce
attack right now. In America, we are still suffering from the af-
tershocks of a controversy over the National Endowment for the
Arts (NEA) funding of an exhibit of Robert Mapplethorpe's controversial erotic photographs. It's not clear if the NEA will survive that scandal. The Cincinnati Arts Center was eventually
acquitted of obscenity charges for hosting the Mapplethorpe exhibit, but don't think that case hasn't had a chilling effect on art
galleries everywhere, especially the smaller ones that do not
have the resources to pay for legal representation.

The Meese Commission on pornography was widely jeered
at when it published its final report in 1986, but the Department
of Justice (DOJ) quietly set about enforcing almost all of its rec-
ommendations for closing down the adult-entertainment industry. The National Obscenity Enforcement Unit changed its
name to the Child Exploitation and Obscenity Section (CEOS),
which makes it much more difficult for politicians to challenge
its activities, even though very little of the unit's energies have
been expended on child pornography, since it hasn't been commercially available in this country since the late seventies.
There are at least ten litigators working at the unit's national
headquarters, and they have appointed assistant U.S. attorneys
specially trained for obscenity prosecution in many of the
ninety-four federal districts under their jurisdiction. They also
utilize the services of the FBI, the IRS, the U.S. Postal Service,
U. S. Customs, and local police departments.

The unit has employed a novel strategy for attacking
pornography. As Nina Reyes reported in *Outweek*, the one hundred and twenty-five convictions they have garnered is no index
of their success because their goal is not necessarily to win a
guilty verdict. Their goal is to put so much pressure on a targeted business that it simply falls apart. A lot more than one

hundred and twenty-five have done so, and a close look at the businesses the DOJ has attacked and their merchandise makes it clear that they have gone after people who were not selling material that a jury would have found to be obscene. The DOJ is more than happy to let a distributor plead guilty to reduced charges, as long as they sign an agreement to stop dealing in X-rated materials. Many do so because they cannot afford lengthy litigation. CEOS has upped the ante by going after directors and even actors in porn films as well as the distribution companies.

Until recently, defending an obscenity case was made even more expensive because charges were filed simultaneously in more than one state. In the case of Phil Harvey, the owner of Adam & Eve, federal Court of Appeals Judge Joyce Hens Green recently issued an injunction that forced the Department of Justice to pursue one case in one venue at a time, but they have asked to have that injunction lifted. Harvey must be an ornery and stubborn guy. He has spent more than two million dollars defending this case. But many businesses find the prospect of facing a long chain of prosecutions every bit as daunting as, say, one in Utah, one in North Carolina, and one in Mississippi.

The Racketeer Influenced and Corrupt Organizations Act (RICO), originally passed in 1970 to fight organized-crime drug syndicates, has also been a powerful tool for smut prosecutors ever since Sen. Jesse Helms (R-NC) won approval to extend it to obscenity in 1984. RICO's definition of a corrupt organization is vague and broad. If federal prosecutors feel that a business qualifies, they have sweeping powers to seize any property or assets that might be linked to the commission of a crime—before conviction! In the case of Ferris Alexander, who owned a chain of adult bookstores and theaters in the Twin Cities, this meant that government agents hauled away more than one hundred thousand books, magazines, and videotapes and burned them even though only thirteen books and tapes were tried for obscenity, and only seven of those items were found to be obscene. The Supreme Court is currently reviewing Alexander's appeal. Even if the high court limits DOJ use of RICO in porn cases, federal prosecutors have cut a swath through the X-rated movie industry that looks like Sherman's march through Georgia.

The Department of Justice has chosen to focus on gay male material and S/M. This smart piece of strategy has created a huge pall of silence from most civil libertarians, who could be counted on to squawk if the feds were busting the risqué stuff they like to read in the bathroom. Magazines featuring even the tamest photos of bondage are becoming harder and harder to find in the U.S. When cops confiscate S/M material, it is invariably described to journalists as "violent pornography." Last time I checked, very few rapes were being committed by women in stiletto heels and leather corsets, but perhaps I live too sheltered a life to really know.

Of course, as publishing and distributing S/M imagery becomes more dangerous, fewer and fewer companies are willing to take chances. Commercial S/M porn is being produced by increasingly sordid companies, many of which are ignorant about the fetish community and simply want to make a quick buck off the weirdos. Production values fall, and the stuff they churn out looks less and less like my fantasies and more and more like Andrea Dworkin's.

Unfortunately, a kind of precedent exists for banning S/M images even if they are not sexually explicit, since the Supreme Court has upheld the constitutionality of banning another category of non-explicit "harmful matter"—that which features minors. An image of a minor need not be sexually explicit to qualify as child pornography. In fact, a jury was recently persuaded to convict a man of possessing child pornography because he owned photographs of children in bathing suits and underwear. The prosecution argued that "the upper inner thigh" constituted a sex organ. If someone can be sent to jail for owning the equivalent of the Sears Roebuck swimsuit section, bull-whips and handcuffs may soon be treated as surrogate genitalia as well.

The National Law Center for Families and Children (NLCFC), an anti-pornography group which acts as a consultant for locales that are writing new sex laws, recently persuaded the town of Oxnard, California to ban the sale of "any device, instrument or paraphernalia designed or marketed primarily for stimulation of the human genital organ...[including] phallic-shaped vibrators, dildoes [sic] [and] non-medical enema kits."

This whimsical bit of blue law was touted as a law against sadomasochistic sex toys. Whips and chains are included in its purview. Presumably it will also become illegal to purchase wooden spoons, plastic clothespins, feather dusters, and leather shoelaces in Oxnard, as well as in other towns lucky enough to hire the NLCFC.

There is no guarantee that the American government's war on pornography will stop just because liberal Democrat Bill Clinton has been elected president. Hillary Clinton is among the women who sent letters of support to Enough is Enough, a new women's group that is rallying liberals and conservatives to the anti-porn cause. Tipper "Over" Gore, founder of the Parents' Music Resource Center, probably won't have herself tied to the railroad tracks to stop this particular train. One of the leaders of the new organization is Dee Jepsen, President Reagan's liaison to women's groups. She says, "Our mission is to greatly reduce sexual violence—to prevent children, men, women and families from becoming victims—by eliminating child pornography and hard-core pornography from the marketplace."

Anti-porn groups may not be able to directly prosecute video stores for renting X-rated tapes, but they do create a social climate where the shop owners are more likely to simply take the tapes off the shelves before their presence is challenged—if the local chief of police (primed by the U.S. Attorney General's enthusiasm for porn-busting) hasn't already sauntered in and said, "I think those tapes are obscene, and if I see them again, I might have you arrested." Censorship operates on extra-legal as well as legal levels.

In Commonwealth countries, where nobody has any First Amendment rights, things are even worse. The Canadian Supreme Court recently upheld a provision in the criminal code which defines "materials which degrade or subordinate women" as obscene. Such materials are banned in Canada because they supposedly incite violence against women. The opinion was written with the assistance of U.S. citizen Catherine MacKinnon of the University of Michigan Law School. MacKinnon is a bosom buddy of Andrea Dworkin. In 1983, they co-authored a law that defined pornography as discrimination against women.

A version of this law was eventually found unconstitutional by the U.S. Supreme Court, but not before it generated anti-smut campaigns in cities all over the U.S. Of course, the first bust to result from MacKinnon's legal brilliance in Canada was at Glad Day, a gay bookshop in Toronto, which got popped for selling a lesbian-produced sex magazine, *Bad Attitude,* which contained a photograph of a woman being penetrated by another woman's gloved hand. So now we know that the Canadian high court thinks safer sex is degrading to women. The December 1992 issue of *On Our Backs* magazine, another lesbian sex periodical, was seized for featuring "bondage." (A model was wrapped in Christmas tree lights.)

As part of their fierce campaign to protect women's rights, the Mounties have also grabbed copies of *Advocate Men, In Touch,* and *Playguy,* gay men's magazines that feature nude male models, but no sexual activity. They also censored safer-sex information which appeared in *Blueboy* magazine, so now we know that when gay men use condoms, they are actually committing violence against women.

My book of erotic short stories, *Macho Sluts,* is involved in a major obscenity trial. Cops seized it at Little Sisters, a queer bookstore in Vancouver. (It doesn't even have any pictures. And it seems to be perfectly safe for straight bookstores to stock *Macho Sluts.*) Canadian Customs has also seized copies of *The Leather Journal,* a news magazine, and the newsletter of an S/M support group, the Society of Janus. The latter seizure was justified as confiscation of "hate literature."

Meanwhile, *Sex* sells briskly at the major bookstore chains in Canada. It would be nice to think that this is evidence of a thaw among Canadian censors. But in fact, this uneven treatment simply makes it clear that the current prosecutions are at least partially motivated by a desire to close down gay and feminist bookstores. Other people—straight people—can talk about gay men and lesbians and define and describe our sexuality, but we must not be allowed to promote, celebrate, or document our own libidos. The cops know they can't shut down Time-Warner. But they can drive Little Sisters and Glad Day into bankruptcy, even if the shops are exonerated by the courts.

In England, London's largest gay bookstore, Gay's the Word, won't even consider selling *Quim,* a British lesbian sex magazine which often includes S/M material. Gay's the Word barely survived a major obscenity trial in 1985. Last year, magazines like Re/Search's *Modern Primitives* that feature photos of piercing were busted for obscenity, and the booksellers were charged. Professional piercer Mr. Sebastian was recently charged with assault for poking permanent holes in paying customers who had queued up for the privilege. The Operation Spanner case is still dragging on, and will probably have to be appealed to the House of Lords and then the European Court of Human Rights. "Operation Spanner" is the code phrase used by Scotland Yard's obscene publications squad for a roundup of twenty-six men, sixteen of whom were eventually found guilty of assault and aiding and abetting assault, because local cops had stumbled across some videotapes of group S/M scenes. Judge Rant ruled that consent was irrelevant. Nor was he swayed by the fact that all defendants were over twenty-one, and none of the sex was commercial. Some defendants received four-year jail sentences. All of them have lost their jobs, and some have attempted suicide because of the negative publicity about the trial.

The same Scotland Yard obscene publications squad also raided the home of performance artist Genesis P-Orridge of the Temple of Psychic Youth. P-Orridge was forced to leave the country after a tabloid television program aired one of the confiscated films (which was rife with gory special effects) and claimed it was a record of genuine satanic child abuse. The entire body of his work is now in police hands, and he dares not go home for fear he and his wife will lose custody of their children.

Even publications far tamer (and prettier) than *Sex* are not safe in England. When someone sent a questionable video to *Skin Two,* a fetish fashion magazine that features absolutely no explicit sex, police stormed their offices. Apparently frustrated because they couldn't find anything illegal on the premises, the bobbies took publisher Tim Woodward home, searched his house, and confiscated some of his personal gear. Perhaps the sex crime being committed here was producing an erotic magazine that doesn't fall apart after the first reading.

Time-Warner and Madonna did not create the sex wars, but it would be nice if some of the millions of dollars that this book is going to make could be funneled into defending its cousins-german. Since Time-Warner picked R.R. Donnelley, a printer which refused to handle Richard Mohr's *Gay Ideas: Outing and Other Controversies* (Beacon Press) and Jack Hart's *Gay Sex: A Manual for Men Who Love Men* (Alyson Publications), I think I'll just go ahead and send out my own checks. But I do hope the people who can afford to buy a copy of *Sex* will send at least an equivalent amount to the defense funds that are trying to keep homegrown, more accurate, hotter S/M material in circulation.

Despite all of this, the S/M community will still find itself in the awkward position of defending *Sex*. The people who want to keep it out of the public libraries and prevent bookstores from selling it are not motivated by a desire to see S/M or any other minority sexual behavior depicted in a more accurate fashion. They don't want any pictures being taken of subversive, radical sex, and they don't really want anybody doing it either. So I've marked the pages in *Sex* that are thrilling: the ecstatic skinhead drinking from a fountain of nameless liquid; a nude Madonna eating pizza, clothed in beauty and power like a Minoan goddess revealing her breasts; the cross-dressed aristocrat who shelters a little blond girl inside her suit jacket like a real dyke daddy; the teeth caught in a tit-ring and the tongue lavishing attention upon a fetish ballet slipper with a seven-inch heel; Madonna straddling a radiator, a spouting fish, and a mirror. I'm going to need a lot of help to get it up for this turn along the barricades.

## ABOUT THE CONTRIBUTORS

**Susie Bright** is the author of *Sexual Reality: A Virtual Sex World Reader* (Cleis Press) and *Susie Sexpert's Lesbian Sex World* (Cleis Press). She edited *Herotica* (Down There Press) and *Herotica II* (Plume) and is a former editor of *On Our Backs*. Her lectures, video presentations and safe sex demos pack theaters in the United States, Canada and Europe.

**Pat Califia**'s essays, poetry and short stories have appeared in *The Advocate, Skin Two, Co-Evolution Quarterly, Frighten the Horses, Taste of Latex,* and *On Our Backs.* Her work has been anthologized in *High Risk* (Amy Scholder and Ira Silverberg, eds., Plume), *Discontents* (Dennis Cooper, ed., Amethyst), *Flesh and the Word* (John Preston, ed., NAL-Dutton), *Leatherfolk* (Mark Thompson, ed., Alyson Publications). Her latest book of short stories is *Melting Point* (Alyson Publications).

**John Champagne** is a writer and scholar whose novels include *The Blue Lady's Hands* (Carol Publishing Group) and *When the Parrot Boy Sings* (Carol Publishing Group). His critical work has appeared in *Boundary 2, CineAction* and in the anthology *A Member of the Family* (ed. John Preston, Dutton). He received his Ph.D. in Critical and Cultural Studies from the University of Pittsburgh in 1993.

**Cathay Che** is an Asian American/Native Hawaiian queer sex-positive activist and artist who lives in New York City. She is currently working on a book of queer Asian theory and fiction, titled *TJG* (Trendy Japanese Girl).

**Douglas Crimp** teaches visual and cultural studies at the University of Rochester and lesbian and gay studies at Sarah Lawrence College. His books include *AIDS: Cultural Analysis/Cultural Activism* (MIT Press), *AIDS DemoGraphics* (Bay Press), and *On the Museum's Ruins* (MIT Press).

**Simon Frith** is Co-Director of the John Logie Baird Centre at the Universities of Strathclyde and Glasgow and the Britbeat columnist of the *Village Voice*. He is presently completing a book on the aesthetics of popular music for Harvard University Press.

**Thomas Allen Harris** is an activist and a cultural warrior whose works as a film/video maker, writer, curator and performance artist explore black, lesbian and gay subjectivity. His films and videos include *Splash, Black Boy* and *All in the Family*.

**bell hooks** is a cultural critic, feminist theorist, writer, the author of five books, most recently *Black Looks: Race and Representation* (South End Press), a collectection of essays, and *The Woman's Mourning Song* (Harlem River Press), a book of poems. She is Professor of Women's Studies at Oberlin College.

**Kirsten Marthe Lentz** studies feminism, sexuality and popular culture in the Literary and Cultural Theory Program at Carnegie Mellon University.

**Carol Queen** is a sex educator and sexuality activist in the San Francisco/Bay area who frequently writes on and always honors marginalized sexualities and sexual diversity.

**Andrew Ross** teaches English and American Studies at Princeton University. His books include *Strange Weather: Culture, Science and Technology in the Age of Limits* (Verso) and *No Respect: Intellectuals and Popular Culture* (Routledge). He is the editor of *Universal Abandon: The Politics of Postmodernism* (University of Minnesota Press) and coeditor of *Technoculture* (University of Minnesota Press) and of the journal *Social Text*.

**Michael Warner** teaches American literature and gay studies at Rutgers University. He is the author of *The Letters of the Republic: Publication and the Public Sphere in Eighteenth-Century America* (Harvard), and editor of *Fear of a Queer Planet: Queer Politics and Social Theory* (University of Minnesota Press). In addition to scholarly essays on subjects ranging from the Puritans ("New English Sodom") to Thoreau ("Thoreau's Bottom"), he contributes essays and reviews to *VLS* and the *Village Voice*.

## BOOKS FROM CLEIS PRESS

### Sexual Politics

*Good Sex: Real Stories from Real People* by Julia Hutton.
ISBN: 0-939416-56-5 24.95 cloth; ISBN: 0-939416-57-3 12.95 paper.

*Madonnarama: Essays on Sex and Popular Culture*
edited by Lisa Frank and Paul Smith.
ISBN: 0-939416-72-7 24.95 cloth; ISBN: 0-939416-71-9 9.95 paper.

*Sex Work: Writings by Women in the Sex Industry* edited by
Frédérique Delacoste and Priscilla Alexander.
ISBN: 0-939416-10-7 24.95 cloth; ISBN: 0-939416-11-5 16.95 paper.

*Susie Bright's Sexual Reality: A Virtual Sex World Reader*
by Susie Bright.
ISBN: 0-939416-58-1 24.95 cloth; ISBN: 0-939416-59-X 9.95 paper.

*Susie Sexpert's Lesbian Sex World* by Susie Bright.
ISBN: 0-939416-34-4 24.95 cloth; ISBN: 0-939416-35-2 9.95 paper.

### Lesbian Studies

*Boomer: Railroad Memoirs* by Linda Niemann.
ISBN: 0-939416-55-7  12.95 paper.

*Different Daughters: A Book by Mothers of Lesbians*
edited by Louise Rafkin.
ISBN: 0-939416-12-3 21.95 cloth; ISBN: 0-939416-13-1 9.95 paper.

*Different Mothers: Sons & Daughters of Lesbians Talk About
Their Lives* edited by Louise Rafkin.
ISBN: 0-939416-40-9 24.95 cloth; ISBN: 0-939416-41-7 9.95 paper.

*A Lesbian Love Advisor* by Celeste West.
ISBN: 0-939416-27-1 24.95 cloth; ISBN: 0-939416-26-3 9.95 paper.

*Long Way Home: The Odyssey of a Lesbian Mother and Her Children* by Jeanne Jullion.
ISBN: 0-939416-05-0 8.95 paper.

*More Serious Pleasure: Lesbian Erotic Stories and Poetry* edited by the Sheba Collective.
ISBN: 0-939416-48-4 24.95 cloth; ISBN: 0-939416-47-6 9.95 paper.

*The Night Audrey's Vibrator Spoke: A Stonewall Riots Collection* by Andrea Natalie.
ISBN: 0-939416-64-6 8.95 paper.

*Queer and Pleasant Danger: Writing Out My Life* by Louise Rafkin.
ISBN: 0-939416-60-3 24.95 cloth; ISBN: 0-939416-61-1 9.95 paper.

*Serious Pleasure: Lesbian Erotic Stories and Poetry* edited by the Sheba Collective.
ISBN: 0-939416-46-8 24.95 cloth; ISBN: 0-939416-45-X 9.95 paper.

## Politics of Health

*The Absence of the Dead Is Their Way of Appearing* by Mary Winfrey Trautmann.
ISBN: 0-939416-04-2 8.95 paper.

*AIDS: The Women* edited by Ines Rieder and Patricia Ruppelt.
ISBN: 0-939416-20-4 24.95 cloth; ISBN: 0-939416-21-2 9.95 paper

*Don't: A Woman's Word* by Elly Danica.
ISBN: 0-939416-23-9 21.95 cloth; ISBN: 0-939416-22-0 8.95 paper

*1 in 3: Women with Cancer Confront an Epidemic* edited by Judith Brady.
ISBN: 0-939416-50-6 24.95 cloth; ISBN: 0-939416-49-2 10.95 paper.

*Unholy Alliances: New Women's Fiction*
edited by Louise Rafkin.
ISBN: 0-939416-14-X 21.95 cloth; ISBN: 0-939416-15-8 9.95 paper.

*The Wall* by Marlen Haushofer.
ISBN: 0-939416-53-0 24.95 cloth;  ISBN: 0-939416-54-9 paper.


## Latin America

*Beyond the Border: A New Age in Latin American Women's Fiction* edited by Nora Erro-Peralta and Caridad Silva-Núñez.
ISBN: 0-939416-42-5 24.95 cloth; ISBN: 0-939416-43-3 12.95 paper.

*The Little School: Tales of Disappearance and Survival in Argentina* by Alicia Partnoy.
ISBN: 0-939416-08-5 21.95 cloth; ISBN: 0-939416-07-7 9.95 paper.

*Revenge of the Apple* by Alicia Partnoy.
ISBN: 0-939416-62-X 24.95 cloth; ISBN: 0-939416-63-8 8.95 paper.

*You Can't Drown the Fire: Latin American Women Writing in Exile* edited by Alicia Partnoy.
ISBN: 0-939416-16-6 24.95 cloth; ISBN: 0-939416-17-4 9.95 paper.


## Autobiography, Biography, Letters

*Peggy Deery: An Irish Family at War* by Nell McCafferty.
ISBN: ISBN: 0-939416-38-7 24.95 cloth; ISBN: 0-939416-39-5 9.95 paper.

*The Shape of Red: Insider/Outsider Reflections* by Ruth Hubbard and Margaret Randall.
ISBN: 0-939416-19-0 24.95 cloth; ISBN: 0-939416-18-2 9.95 paper.

*Women & Honor: Some Notes on Lying* by Adrienne Rich.
ISBN: 0-939416-44-1 3.95 paper.

*Voices in the Night: Women Speaking About Incest*
edited by Toni A.H. McNaron and Yarrow Morgan.
ISBN: 0-939416-02-6 9.95 paper.

*With the Power of Each Breath: A Disabled Women's Anthology* edited by Susan Browne, Debra Connors and Nanci Stern.
ISBN: 0-939416-09-3 24.95 cloth; ISBN: 0-939416-06-9 10.95 paper.

*Woman-Centered Pregnancy and Birth*
by the Federation of Feminist Women's Health Centers.
ISBN: 0-939416-03-4 11.95 paper.

### Fiction

*Another Love* by Erzsébet Galgóczi.
ISBN: 0-939416-52-2 24.95 cloth; ISBN: 0-939416-51-4 8.95 paper.

*Cosmopolis: Urban Stories by Women* edited by Ines Rieder.
ISBN: 0-939416-36-0 24.95 cloth; ISBN: 0-939416-37-9 9.95 paper.

*A Forbidden Passion* by Cristina Peri Rossi.
ISBN: 0-939416-64-0 24.95 cloth; ISBN: 0-939416-68-9 9.95 paper.

*In the Garden of Dead Cars* by Sybil Claiborne.
ISBN: 0-939416-65-4 24.95 cloth; ISBN: 0-939416-66-2 9.95 paper.

*Night Train To Mother* by Ronit Lentin.
ISBN: 0-939416-29-8 24.95 cloth; ISBN: 0-939416-28-X 9.95 paper.

*The One You Call Sister: New Women's Fiction*
edited by Paula Martinac.
ISBN: 0-939416-30-1 24.95 cloth; ISBN: 0-939416031-X 9.95 paper.

*Only Lawyers Dancing* by Jan McKemmish.
ISBN: 0-939416-70-0 24.95 cloth; ISBN: 0-939416-69-7 9.95 paper.

## Animal Rights

*And a Deer's Ear, Eagle's Song and Bear's Grace:*
*Relationships Between Animals and Women*
edited by Theresa Corrigan and Stephanie T. Hoppe.
ISBN: 0-939416-38-7 24.95 cloth; ISBN: 0-939416-39-5 9.95 paper.

*With a Fly's Eye, Whale's Wit and Woman's Heart:*
*Relationships Between Animals and Women*
edited by Theresa Corrigan and Stephanie T. Hoppe.
ISBN: 0-939416-24-7 24.95 cloth; ISBN: 0-939416-25-5 9.95 paper.

Since 1980, Cleis Press has published progressive books by
women. We welcome your order and will ship your books as
quickly as possible. Individual orders must be prepaid (U.S.
dollars only). Please add 15% shipping. PA residents add 6%
sales tax. Mail orders: Cleis Press, PO Box 8933, Pittsburgh PA
15221. MasterCard and Visa orders: include account number,
exp. date, and signature. FAX your credit card order: (412) 937-
1567. Or, phone us Mon-Fri, 9am –5pm EST: (412) 937-1555.

## ABOUT THE EDITORS

**Lisa Frank** is Publicity Director at Cleis Press and teaches cultural studies at Carlow College.

**Paul Smith** teaches at Carnegie Mellon University. He is the author of *Clint Eastwood: A Cultural Production* (University of Minnesota Press) as well as many articles on contemporary culture and cultural theory. He is the editor, with Alice Jardine, of *Men in Feminism* (Methuen).